Ready-to-Use
LEARNING
DISABILITIES
Activities Kit

Ready-to-Use
LEARNING
DISABILITIES
Activities Kit

Joan M. Harwell

**THE CENTER FOR APPLIED
RESEARCH IN EDUCATION**
West Nyack, New York 10995

10 9 8 7 6 5 4 3 2 1

Library of Congress Cataloging-in-Publication Data
Harwell, Joan M., 1936–
    Ready-to-use learning disabilities activities kit / Joan M.
Harwell.
        p. cm.
    ISBN 0–87628–846–8
    1. Learning disabled children—Education (Primary)—United States.
2. Teaching—Aids and devices. 3. Reading (Primary)—United States.
4. Language arts (Primary)—United States. 5. Mathematics—study
and teaching (Primary)—United States. 6. Education, Primary—
United States—Activity programs. I. Center for Applied Research
in Education. II. Title.
LC4705.H37 1993
371.3′078—dc20   92–43838
                                                                                CIP

ISBN 0-87628-846-8

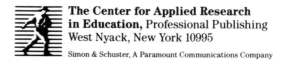
**The Center for Applied Research
in Education,** Professional Publishing
West Nyack, New York 10995
Simon & Schuster, A Paramount Communications Company

Printed in the United States of America

ABOUT THE AUTHOR

Joan M. Harwell has over 25 years of experience as a regular classroom teacher and special education teacher for educationally handicapped children in the public schools of San Bernardino, California. She has developed and taught several successful remedial programs for slow and reluctant learners and is the author of *How to Diagnose and Correct Learning Difficulties in the Classroom* (Parker Publishing Company, 1982) and *Complete Learning Disabilities Handbook: Ready-to-Use Techniques for Teaching Learning Handicapped Students* (The Center, 1989).

Ms. Harwell earned a B.A. degree from San Jose State College and an M.A. from the University of Redlands.

ABOUT THIS RESOURCE

The *Ready-to-Use Learning Disabilities Activities Kit* is designed to help regular and special teachers of elementary children in the areas of reading, language arts, and math. It gives the busy teacher over 200 reproducible activities for quickly and effectively meeting the needs of students who have a wide range of functional levels.

The materials in the *Kit* are not intended to be a comprehensive program but rather a supplement to the materials and course of study recommended by your district. For example, obviously the math materials are limited to those that develop critical thinking skills by helping students visualize what words and numbers mean.

The activities are presented by approximate grade level, kindergarten to 2.9, but you will find yourself moving back and forth from unit to unit as you seek to meet each student's needs:

- Unit One, "Pre-Academics for Young Learning Disabled Students," provides activities appropriate for Head Start and kindergarten-aged children whose learning disabilities render them not yet ready for beginning academics.
- Unit Two, "Beginning Academics," presents activities appropriate for children who are functioning at grades 1.0 to 1.9.
- Unit Three, "Moving 'Write' Along," offers activities for children who are functioning in the 2.0 to 2.9 range.

While these materials were created for use with learning disabled children, they may be used with youngsters in the general school population as well. You could, for example, use the activities as homework for regular class students, giving pre-academics to beginning first graders, first-grade materials as homework for second graders, and so on.

The activities at each level are preceded by a general discussion of the learning objectives and prerequisites at that level and specific suggestions for using each of the activities that follow.

I hope that you find the *Ready-to-Use Learning Disabilities Activities Kit* a valuable tool for working with your students.

Joan M. Harwell

CONTENTS

Objectives • Rationales • Directions for Activity Sheets
   • Extension

Activity Sheets

1–1   Nursery Rhymes (Humpty Dumpty)
1–1   Nursery Rhymes (Hickory Dickory Dock)
1–1   Nursery Rhymes (Jack Be Nimble)
1–1   Nursery Rhymes (Little Bo Peep)
1–1   Nursery Rhymes (Wee Willie Winkie)
1–1   Nursery Rhymes (Little Boy Blue)

Other Useful Nursery Rhymes

Unit Two
BEGINNING ACADEMICS • 71

Objective 1 • Rationale • Directions • Lesson Plan for
Days 1–20 • Letter to Parents

Activity Sheets

2–1A Sounds List
2–1A Sounds List (student response sheet)

Lesson Plan for Days 11–30 • Objective 2   Rationale
• Directions • Lesson Plan for Days 30–40

Activity Sheets

2–1B Alphabet Cards (a–i)
2–1B Alphabet Cards (j–r)
2–1B Alphabet Cards (s–z)
2–1B Sounds Cards (a–i)
2–1B Sounds Cards (j–r)
2–1B Sounds Cards (s–z)

Objective 3 • Rationale • Directions • Objective 4
• Rationale • Lesson Plan for Days 40–60 • Directions

Activity Sheets

2–1C Vowel Bulletin Board (a in apple)
2–1C Vowel Bulletin Board (e in edge)
2–1C Vowel Bulletin Board (i in itch)
2–1C Vowel Bulletin Board (o in octopus)
2–1C Vowel Bulletin Board (u in up)

Activity Sheets

Objective   •   Rationale   •   Directions for Activity Sheets

Activity Sheets

Objective 1   •   Rationale   •   Directions for Activity Sheets
•   Objective 2   •   Rationale

Activity Sheets

**Unit Three
MOVING "WRITE" ALONG   •   161**

3–13 COMPREHENSION **218**

Objective 1 • Rationale • Objective 2 • Rationale
• Extension

Activity Sheets

3–13 Comprehension (2.0)
3–13 Comprehension (2.0)
3–13 Comprehension (2.0)
3–13 Comprehension (2.5)
3–13 Comprehension (2.5)
3–13 Comprehension (2.5)
3–13 Comprehension (2.5)
3–13 Comprehension (2.5)—Pictures to Cut Out
3–13 Comprehension (2.5)—Pictures to Cut Out

3–14 WRITING PARAGRAPHS **228**

Objective • Rationale • Directions

Activity Sheets

3–14 Writing Paragraphs—Notebook Materials
3–14 Writing Paragraphs—Set I (The Kite)
3–14 Writing Paragraphs—Set I (My Friend)
3–14 Writing Paragraphs—Set I (The Baby Birds)
3–14 Writing Paragraphs—Set I (A New Book)
3–14 Writing Paragraphs—Set II
3–14 Writing Paragraphs—Set II ("Saturdays")
3–14 Writing Paragraphs—Set II ("Jan's Bread")
3–14 Writing Paragraphs—Set II ("Making Bread")
3–14 Writing Paragraphs—Set II ("Scared")
3–14 Writing Paragraphs—Set II ("Hide and Seek")
3–14 Writing Paragraphs—Set III (Alone)
3–14 Writing Paragraphs—Set III (Vacation)
3–14 Writing Paragraphs—Set III (Animal Homes)
3–14 Writing Paragraphs—Set III (A Walk in the Woods)
3–14 Writing Paragraphs—Set III (Angry)
3–14 Writing Paragraphs—Set IV (Lost Dog/Found Dog)
3–14 Writing Paragraphs—Set IV (Racing)
3–14 Writing Paragraphs—Set IV (Our New Pet)

Ready-to-Use
LEARNING
DISABILITIES
Activities Kit

UNIT 1

Pre-Academics
for Young Learning
Disabled Children

Preparing Children for First Grade—
Skills to Be Taught

For a child to benefit from the first-grade educational experience, he or she needs the following skills:

1. Ability to follow three simple directions
2. Vocabulary development sufficient to express himself or herself and understand others
3. Ability to recognize colors
4. Ability to classify items that belong together
5. Ability to associate items that relate to each other
6. Ability to recognize likenesses and differences in pictures, letters, and words
7. Ability to recognize the letters of the lowercase and uppercase alphabet and to say the alphabet in proper sequence
8. Ability to sit and follow instructions for a period of 10 minutes
9. Ability to hold the pencil correctly and to make deliberate marks (can copy simple shapes), draw simple pictures, and make letters
10. Ability to use scissors and glue correctly

Activities suggested to develop these skills include

Easel Art   Begin with one color; later, use two. The value of the activity markedly increases when an older person (cross-age tutor, parent, aide) is near at hand to say, "Oh, you're using red" or "You've made a circle" or "Tell me about your picture."

Puzzles   Begin with the wood ones of only 3 to 9 pieces. Later move to the 25-piece type.

1. Have the student separate pieces with a flat side from curved pieces (you will want to stay with the child and give help as he or she does this).
2. Next have the student locate the four corners (they are the ones with two flat sides).
3. Using the picture on the box as a guide, have the student place the four corners on the table (you will need to give help so he or she gets them at "top/left," "top/right," "bottom/left," etc.).
4. Using color, help the child build the frame first and work inward.

Blocks   Children need a wide variety of block shapes and sizes. The "Can you do this?" game works well with young children. You build a figure; then have the student build a figure, comparing yours to his or hers at each step.
Praise accomplishment; give guidance as needed.

Picture Books   Several times daily children need exposure to picture books. Have an adult sitting near at hand to a group of three. As you read, focus each child's attention with questions such as, "What is this?" "Can you find a ball?" or "What is she doing?" "What do you think is being said?" Give children help in identifying objects.

Coloring, Cutting, Gluing   Young children require lots of practice to master these skills. This book has many activities throughout the lower grades that involve these three skills.

Music   Young children love to use simple instruments (drums, cymbals, gourds) and like rhythm activities.

Paper-and-Pencil Activities   You will find a number of pencil-and-paper activities in the next section to supplement those your district supplies.

1–1 NURSERY RHYMES

Objective 1: The student will be able to repeat 11 nursery rhymes verbatim.

Rationale: Nursery rhymes are a part of our cultural base—that common body of knowledge to which we are all exposed. Many of the rhymes date back centuries. For example, Ole King Cole was supposed to have been a popular king who ruled England about A.D. 200. Jack Horner was a steward to King Henry VIII who carried valuable papers in a pie for safety.

Nursery rhymes can be used to extend the child's language development as well as his or her knowledge about the world. To illustrate, the rhyme "Rub-a-Dub-Dub" contains the word knave. This is an ideal time to explain that a knave is a rascal, or a rogue, or a scamp. Of course, if these words are not known to children, you will need to think of current examples to explain how a scamp behaves. Choose characters that the children see on TV or relate it to incidences that happen in children's lives. One which all children seem to understand is "a rascal is a person who is doing something he or she should not be doing." Ask them to relate an experience when they did something their parent told them not to do. After they relate their experience, say "That was a knavish act" or "What a scamp you were" or "You were being a little rascal."

In the "Old Woman in the Shoe," you have a chance to explain "broth," meaning the watery part of the soup. This rhyme offers the opportunity to discuss spanking, which affords the ideal chance to talk about what the child needs to do to avoid punishment.

When the nursery rhymes are accompanied by delightful pictures and teacher explanations, children can learn much about the beauty of our language.

Upon first exposure, our goal is to familiarize children with these rhymes by going over them many times. For most children, memorization occurs naturally as the child hears the rhymes.

Children enjoy acting out some rhymes. They will laugh uproariously at the thought of "Jack Be Nimble" burning his fanny on that candlestick. This enactment can lead to discussions on fire safety (not playing with matches).

Once a child becomes very familiar with several rhymes, you can move on to the next objective.

Objective 2: The student will show an awareness of rhyming words. When you say a word, he or she will give a rhyming word.

4

Rationale: Understanding that words rhyme will be helpful later when the child begins to spell.

As you read "Humpty Dumpty" for the 20th time, stop and let the children give the words <u>wall</u> and <u>fall</u>. You may even want to call to their attention that these words are similar (the "all").

Objective 3: The student will demonstrate his or her understanding of tracking by moving his or her finger left to right as you jointly read a rhyme.

Rationale: Being aware that we read from left to right is an essential prereading skill. Nursery rhymes make an excellent vehicle for teaching this skill.

With the child sitting next to you, help him or her move his or her finger as you read. Most children will acquire this skill quickly.

Directions for Activity Sheets: Read each verse aloud to the child. Help the child move his or her finger from left to right as you read.

Extension: Help the children make their activity sheets into booklets to take home. Encourage them to "read the rhymes to younger brothers and sisters." Being able to do this gives them a real sense of power and enhances their self-esteem.

Humpty Dumpty

Humpty Dumpty sat on a <u>wall</u>,
Humpty Dumpty had a great <u>fall</u>;
All the King's horses
And all the King's men
Couldn't put Humpty together again.

1–1 NURSERY RHYMES

Name _____

Hickory Dickory Dock

Hickory Dickory <u>Dock</u>!
The mouse ran up the <u>clock</u>.
The clock struck one,
And down he did run,
Hickory Dickory Dock!

1–1 NURSERY RHYMES

Name _____

Jack Be Nimble

Jack be nimble,
Jack be <u>quick</u>,
Jack jump over
The candle <u>stick</u>.

1–1 NURSERY RHYMES

Little Bo Peep

Little Bo <u>Peep</u>
Has lost her <u>sheep</u>,
And doesn't know where
   to find them.
Leave them alone,
And they'll come home,
Wagging their tails
   behind them.

Name _____

Wee Willie Winkie

Wee Willie Winkie runs
   through the <u>town</u>,
Upstairs, downstairs,
   in his night <u>gown</u>;
Rapping at the windows,
   crying through the <u>lock</u>,
"Are the children in their beds?
For it now is eight <u>o'clock</u>."

1–1 NURSERY RHYMES

Name _____

Little Boy Blue

Little Boy Blue
Come blow your <u>horn</u>!
Sheep's in the meadow,
Cow's in the <u>corn</u>.
Where is the boy who looks
    after the <u>sheep</u>?
He's under the haystack,
    fast a<u>sleep</u>.

Other Useful Nursery Rhymes

Rub-a-dub-dub
Three men in a tub,
Who do you think they be?
The butcher, the baker,
The candlestick maker.
Turn them out,
They're knaves all three.

Old Mother Hubbard
Went to the cupboard
To get her poor dog a bone.
When she got there
The cupboard was bare
So the poor dog got none.

Little Jack Horner,
Sat in a corner,
Eating his Christmas pie;
He stuck in his thumb
And pulled out a plum
And said, "What a good boy am I."

There was an old woman
who lived in a shoe;
She had so many children,
she didn't know what to do.
She gave them some broth
without any bread,
Then spanked them all soundly
and put them to bed.

Curly Locks! Curly Locks! Wilt thou be mine?
Thou shalt not wash dishes nor feed the swine;
But sit on a cushion and sew a fine seam
And feed upon strawberries, sugar, and cream.

1–2 COLORING LARGE OBJECTS

Objective: The student will gain control of the crayon, holding it properly and moving it purposefully.

Rationale: Many children arrive at school with little coloring experience. The kindergarten teacher must move the child from the scribbling stage to being able to hold the pencil and make letters and designs. For children who are still at the scribbling stage, large objects are better.

Directions for Activity Sheets: Have the child outline the object and then color inward with tiny strokes.

Extension: These activity sheets can provide an opportunity to discuss topics such as going to the beach, the difference between chickens and ducks, kinds of bird habitats, or allowing for inferences about what might be in the box. Today's children desperately need to do more talking with adults. According to a 1984 research study, the average child communicates with adults about 2 minutes a day (1 minute with the parent and 1 minute with the teacher).

While children are coloring, it is natural to move from child to child asking each to relate to the picture from his or her own experience with questions such as, "Have you been to the beach? Tell me about it."

Name _____

1–2 COLORING LARGE OBJECTS

Name _____

1–2 COLORING LARGE OBJECTS

Name _____

1–2 COLORING LARGE OBJECTS

Name _____

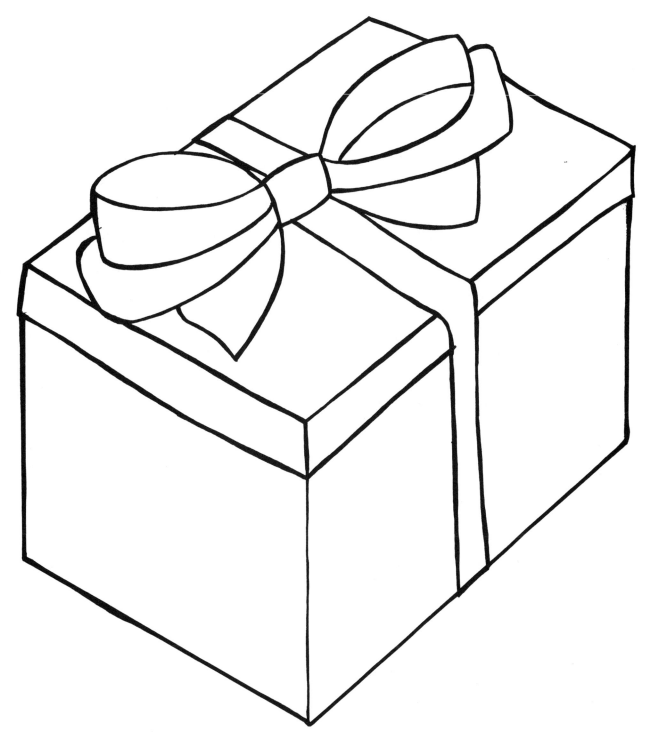

1–2 COLORING LARGE OBJECTS

Name _____

1–2 COLORING LARGE OBJECTS

Name _____

1–2 COLORING LARGE OBJECTS

19

1–3 LISTENING TO
AND FOLLOWING DIRECTIONS

Objective: The child will convert words into mental images and demonstrate that he or she is doing so by marking an activity sheet correctly.

Rationale: This is an activity that a child must be able to do. All through school, teachers will use dittoes, worksheets, and activity sheets to assess what the child is learning. Now that the nursery rhymes are familiar to him or her, they can be used to teach the beginning test-taking skill.

Directions for Activity Sheets: As you read a nursery rhyme, such as "Humpty Dumpty," the child will look at the pictures on the first activity sheet. When you read "sat on a wall," show the child (this can be done with a group using the overhead projector and an exact copy of the worksheet) how to circle the picture of the wall.

If a child fails to mark an object mentioned in the rhyme, stand very close to the child and reread the rhyme, overemphasizing the word you want him or her to hear. If the child still fails to mark the object, it may be that he or she does not know the name of the object. Point to the picture you want marked and say, "This is a wall."

Extension: A second activity that helps children follow directions involves the recognition of shapes and colors. Cut 4-inch circles, squares, and triangles from red, green, and yellow paper. Lay them out on the table. Have the child classify them by shape ("Put all the circles together," etc). Ask the child to hand you a "green circle" or a "red triangle." In doing this activity, the child must hold two concepts (color and shape) in his or her memory. If the child has difficulty doing this, teach him or her to repeat your request before he or she tries to execute it.

As the child shows mastery for this activity, you can begin to add circles, squares, and triangles of other colors. When proficient with all colors, you can add the rectangle. Later, you can add the concepts of large and small by asking the child to hand you a "small yellow rectangle" or a "large purple square."

Some children have trouble with learning color names. You can help by having them associate the color name with an item that is that color. For example,

"Red as fire"

"Green as grass"

"Blue as the sky"

"Black as night"
"Brown as mud"
"Yellow as a banana"
"Orange as an orange"
"Purple as grape juice"
"Pink as cotton candy"
"White as snow"

Name _____

Humpty Dumpty

Little Boy Blue

Wee Willie Winkie

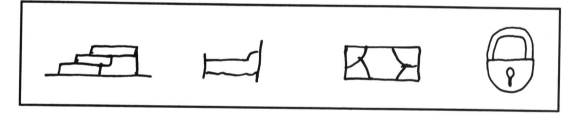

Little Jack Horner

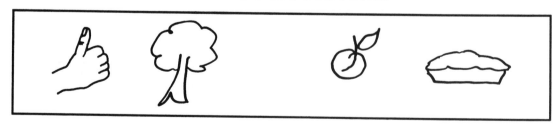

1–3 LISTENING TO AND FOLLOWING DIRECTIONS

Name _____

Old Woman in the Shoe

Rub-a-Dub-Dub

Curly Locks

Old Mother Hubbard

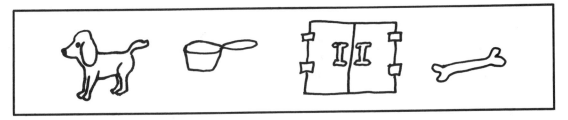

1–3 LISTENING TO AND FOLLOWING DIRECTIONS

Name _____

Directions: Put an X on each thing you can eat.

1–3 LISTENING TO AND FOLLOWING DIRECTIONS

Name _____

Directions: Put an X on each animal.

1–3 LISTENING TO AND FOLLOWING DIRECTIONS

1–4 LIKENESSES/DIFFERENCES

Objective: The student will show an alertness to visual detail demonstrated by the ability to match like designs.

Rationale: In order to read, children must be able to note small differences in words (e.g., <u>three</u> versus <u>there</u>). Many children come to school with little awareness of visual detail. The activity sheets in this section are designed to help develop an alertness to subtle differences.

If you have the time to do the first page one on one with the child, showing him or her how to mark the answer and discussing what makes each picture different from the model, the child usually can do the following sheets as seatwork or homework.

Directions for Activity Sheets: Have the child look at the figure on the left side of the page. Then have the child locate the matching figure on the right side of the page. (If errors are made, help the child understand by showing him or her what is different.)

Extension: As you read books with children, have them carefully examine the pictures for visual detail.

Ask them to tell you "What is happening in this picture?" You may need to tell them that the main theme is generally shown in the foreground or involves the larger figures because children sometimes get caught up in an obscure detail you may not even have noticed and one that is not relevant to the story. This open discussion also provides opportunities for conversation and relating pictures to their personal experience.

Name _____

put	dut	but	put
+ – =	+ – =	+ = –	– = +
snow	snou	snov	snow
2345	2354	2345	2354
cat	CaT	CAT	cat

1–4 LIKENESSES/DIFFERENCES

ept	**eat**	**ept**
CD	**CD**	**Cᗡ**

1–4 LIKENESSES/DIFFERENCES

UM	UW	UM	NM
are	are	ore	rae
was	wsa	saw	was

Name _____

O	**O**	**O**	**O**
b	**d**	**b**	**d**
u	**u**	**n**	**n**
Z.	**.Z**	**Z**	**Z.**
bud	**bun**	**but**	**bud**

1–4 **LIKENESSES/DIFFERENCES**

Name _____

1–5 UNDERSTANDING PATTERNS

Objective: The child will become aware of patterns and will demonstrate this awareness by constructing a pattern while looking at a model.

Rationale: Many educational tasks involve understanding patterns. At the readiness level we have to develop the concept of pattern so that when the child encounters them, he or she recognizes them as patterns (examples include counting by two's, five's, and ten's; multiples; and even the format of a paragraph).

Directions for Activity Sheets: Using the overhead projector and the activity sheets in this section, talk about patterns and how they repeat. Have the children draw on their worksheet as you draw on the overhead. You will find that the children will need a lot of help to do this, so it is advisable to have older helpers to assist them with this activity. These worksheets are not appropriate for homework or independent seatwork.

Extension: Look around your school for additional devices to use in developing pattern awareness. Tangrams, parquetry blocks, and TryTask™ are commonly available. Children enjoy these manipulatives.

1–5 UNDERSTANDING PATTERNS

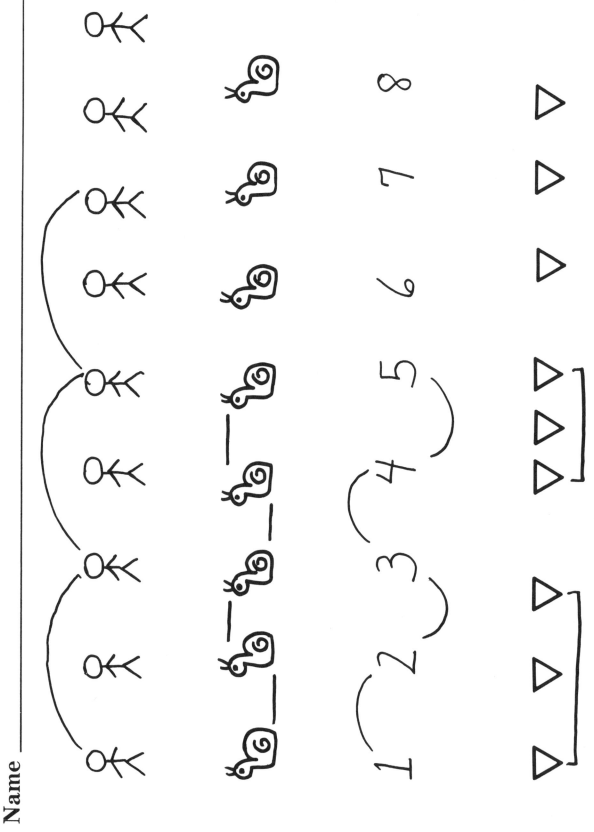

1–5 UNDERSTANDING PATTERNS

Name _____

Directions: Complete each pattern.

oxx	oxx	oxx	___
big	pig	fig	w ___
12	123	1234	___
(people figures)	(bowtie figures)	(snail figures)	(ball figure) ___
bd	bdf	bdfh	___

1-6 TRACING

Objective: The student will hold a crayon/pencil correctly and follow the dashed lines.

Rationale: Being able to hold a crayon or pencil and to move it purposefully are necessary prewriting skills. Some children will arrive at kindergarten without ever having held a crayon or pencil. Others will be at the scribbling stage. A few may be able to color fairly proficiently and write their names. The activity sheets found in this section are designed to help those who have had little or no experience with a writing implement. A child who lacks experience with crayons or pencils can benefit from using a given worksheet more than once. With encouragement, his or her performance generally improves with each exposure.

When you decide it is time to teach letter formation, it is helpful if you can arrange to have an older child or adult sit with each student to ensure that the student is holding his or her pencil correctly. If left alone in the early stages of writing, some children will find unique ways to hold the pencil. This sometimes becomes a problem later because their hand fatigues quickly and by fourth grade they are not able to produce the assigned volume of written work in the allotted time frame.

Likewise, it is important that letters be formed properly. Letters should "Begin at the top of the dot" and "Move downward" or "In the direction indicated by the arrow." Learning correct letter formation improves legibility, speeds up the writing, and makes the transition to cursive easier.

Children need multiple exposures to producing a given letter. Most school districts provide kindergarten teachers with sufficient materials to meet this need.

Directions for Activity Sheets: Have the child trace along the dashed lines with a crayon or a pencil.

Extension: If you have access to tracing paper, you will find that children who are proficient in tracing often enjoy copying pictures from coloring books. This can be a nice seatwork activity for those students.

Name _____

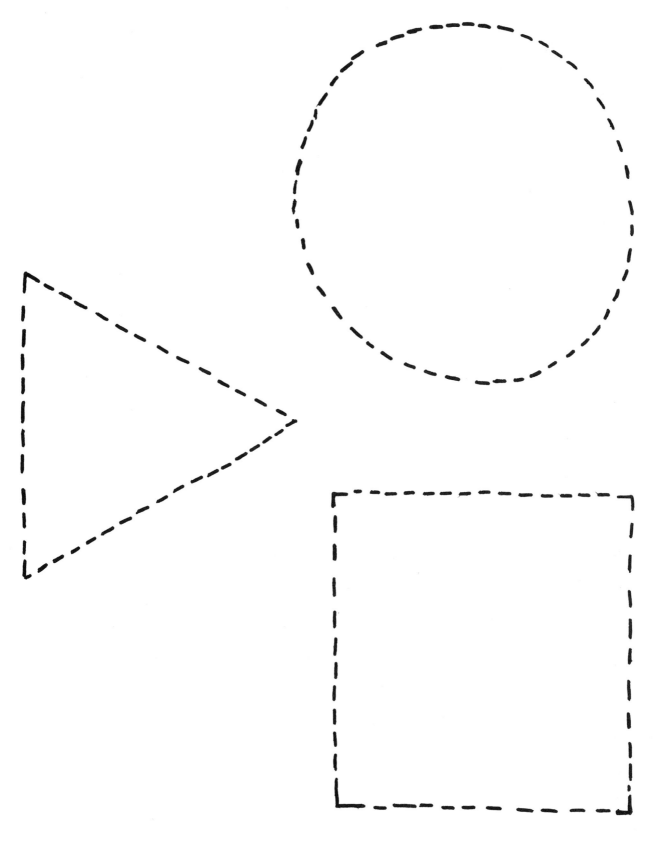

begin

1–6 TRACING

Name _____

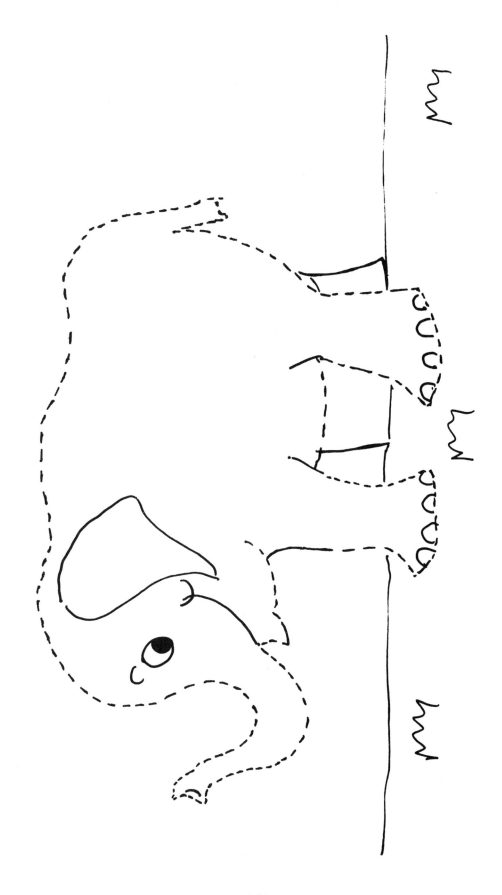

Name _____

1–6 TRACING

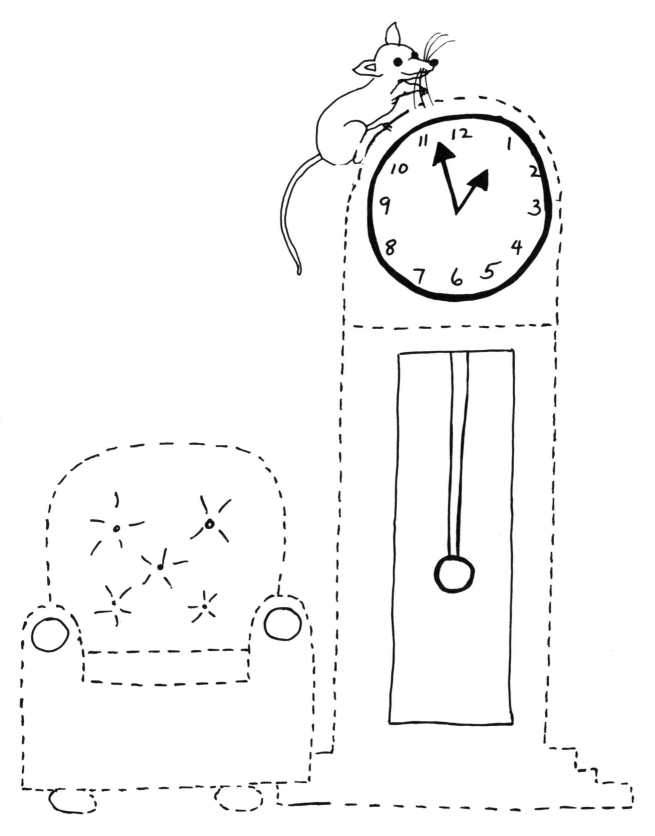

1–6 TRACING

begin

1–6 TRACING

a   j   s

b   k   t

c   l   u

d   m   v

e   n   w

f   o   x

g   p   y

h   qu   z

i   r

1–6 TRACING

1–6 TRACING

1–7 PICTURE COMPLETION

Objective: Given a picture of a familiar object or thing that is missing a portion or part, the student will draw the missing part.

Rationale: Picture completion is another activity that helps youngsters show an awareness of detail, see patterns, and develop skill in making their pencils go where they want them to go. In addition, the concept of symmetry can be introduced. Students often like to do these worksheets more than once, striving for improvement in their production.

Extension: Again the opportunity for vocabulary development should not be overlooked. For example, in talking about the pictures, words such as insect can be used interchangeably with bug and clapper for ding-dong can be introduced.

Name _____

Directions: Finish drawing each picture.

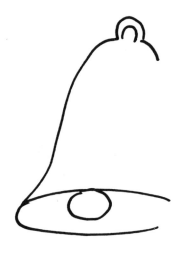

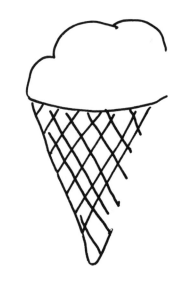

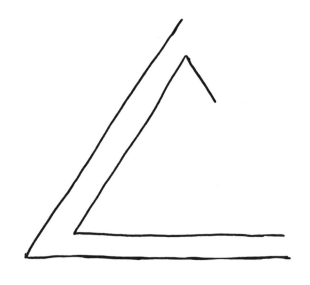

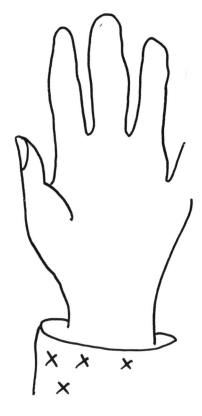

1–7 PICTURE COMPLETION

Name _____

Directions: Finish drawing each picture.

Name _____

Directions: Finish drawing each picture.

1–7 PICTURE COMPLETION

Name _____

Directions: Finish drawing each picture.

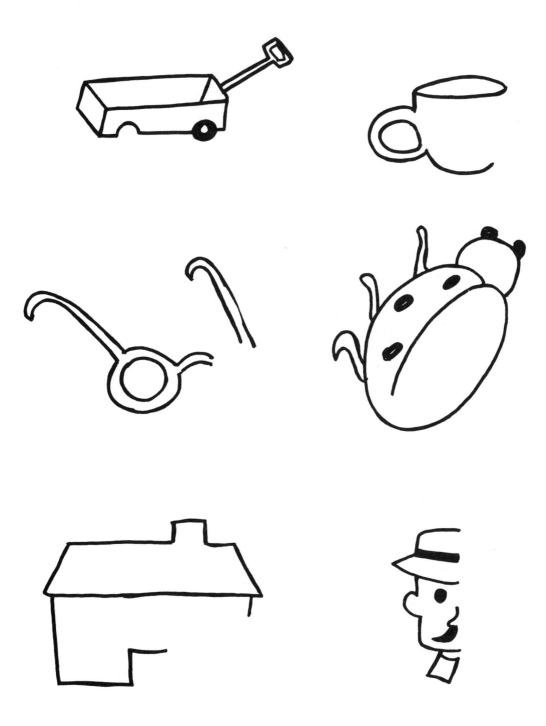

1–8 DIRECTIONALITY

Objective: The child will trace over a given pattern and then reproduce it, using the dots given on the worksheet (model stays in view).

Rationale: These activities help the child to get control of his or her pencil and see patterns. The concepts of "left," "right," "up," and "down" can be advanced if an older person sits with the student and talks him or her through each worksheet.

These activities are particularly useful in spotting children who have learning disabilities. Children with visual perceptual deficits find these activity sheets difficult but, with practice and close supervision, will make improvement in doing them.

Directions for Activity Sheets: Have the child trace over the figure at the left. Using the dots at the right, have the child try to reproduce the figure.

Extension: Some children have difficulty remembering which direction is "right." They can sometimes straighten this out if they are reminded that "they write with their right hand." (The use of the homophones right and write seems to help them.)

There is a song and musical game, called "The Hokey-Pokey," that can be a lot of fun and that also teaches "left" and "right." If you don't know it, ask around. Colleagues will teach it to you and a local music store probably can supply a record of the tune.

Name _____

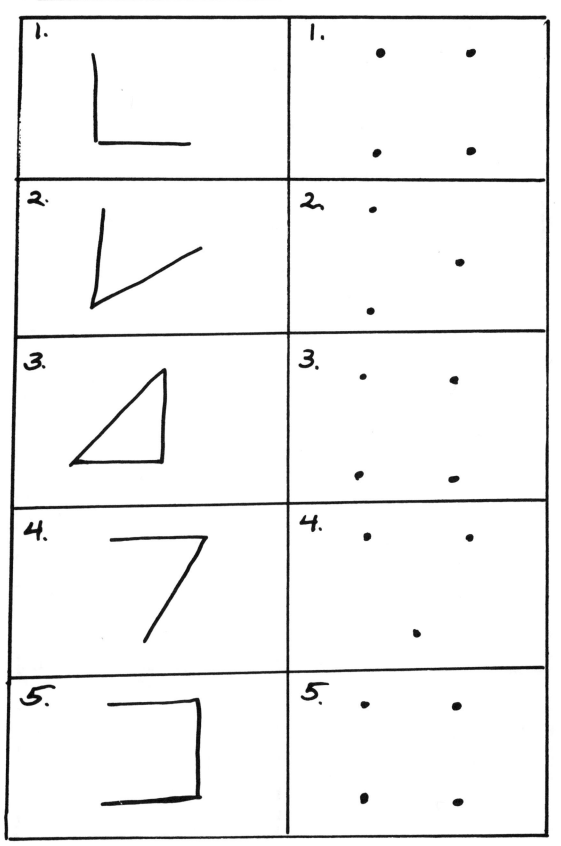

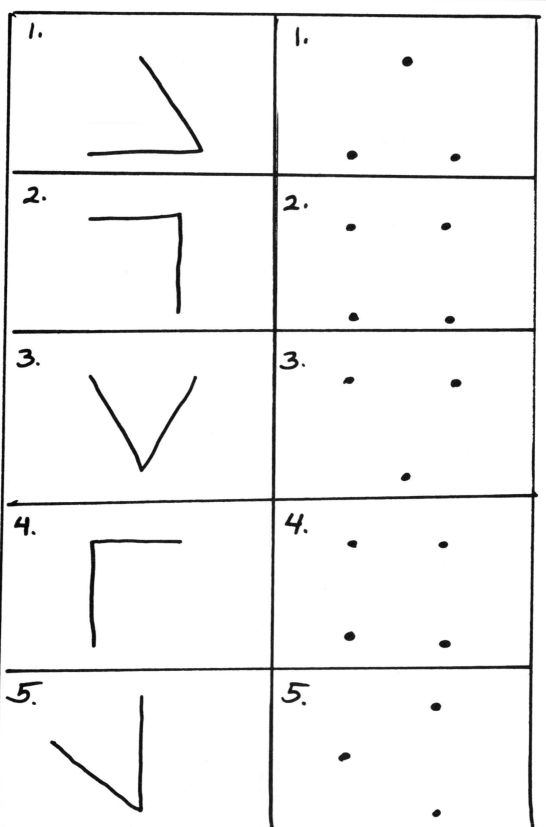

1–8 DIRECTIONALITY

Name _____

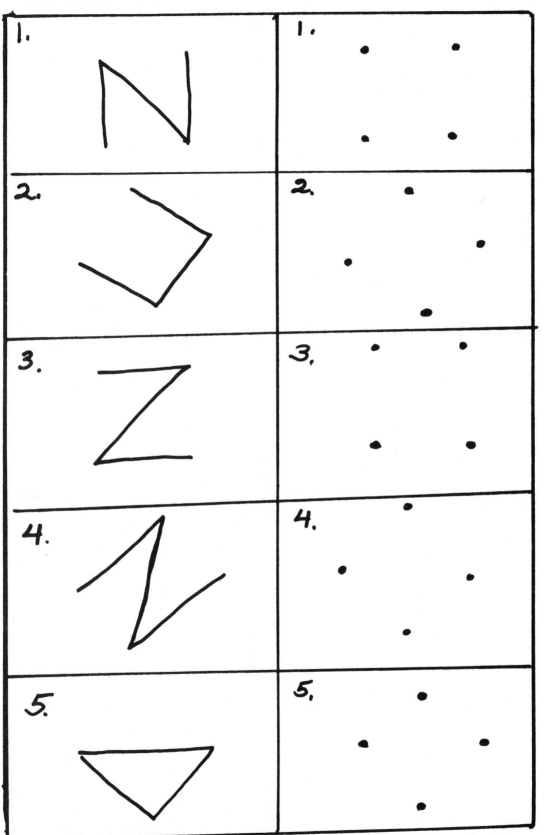

1–8 DIRECTIONALITY

1.	1.
2.	2.
3.	3.
4.	4.
5.	5.

1–8 DIRECTIONALITY

1–9 CLASSIFICATION

Objective: The student will name and group objects that have a similar use—toys, clothing, food, and tools.

Rationale: Classification is a life skill. "A place for everything and everything in its place" was the adage taught by my mother. In the rush of modern life, classification skills can help us locate items we want quickly—socks in this drawer, underwear in that one.

Directions for Activity Sheets: In this section there are three worksheets. Have the child cut out the pictures on all three, placing them in a box. On day 1, ask the child to select all the toys. Have the child show you what he or she has selected. The child places the cutouts on paper and can then glue them. On day 2, the child selects all the items of clothing. Check the child's selections before he or she glues them. On day 3, let the children find and glue all the items that are food. On day 4, there will only be tools left.

Extension: This lesson can be a "gold mine" in terms of language development. Children enjoy telling about their experiences using tools. Learning the names of the tools makes an interesting lesson. If possible, bring in the hammer, pliers, shovel, and hoe, and develop safe ways for the student to use them. Because safety is a primary concern, close supervision is recommended. The uses of chisels, axes, and other instruments can be shown, but care must be exercised to prevent student access to them.

1–9 CLASSIFICATION

1–9 CLASSIFICATION

1–9 CLASSIFICATION

1–10 ASSOCIATION

Objective: The student will be able to match objects that are used together and tell how they are related.

Rationale: These activity sheets provide children with another chance to speak. Therefore, they are best used in small groups of four so each child can answer a question.

Directions for Activity Sheets: Have the children draw a line to show which items go together. Have the children tell why the items are related.

Answers:

key—opens door
pole—catches fish
hammer—hits nail
boots—cover feet

stamp—goes on letter
bird—lays eggs in nest
spade—digs ground for
   planting flower
mitten—warms hands
lamp shade—covers light
   bulb

leaf—grows on tree
rose—goes in vase
toothbrush—needs paste
   to clean teeth
lid—covers pan
plug—goes in socket

tub—associates with towel
   after bath
engine—runs on a track
baby—sleeps in crib
bug—visits flowers

trap—catches mice
cap—is worn when
   playing baseball
matches—set fire
fork—is used for eating
   (just as spoon is)
mop—is used with pail to
   clean the floor

Extension: Out of this activity you can spin off many important mini-lessons. Words like socket will be new to a majority of your students. You will find that they may or may not know there is electricity behind the wall.

Name _____

Directions: Draw a line to show which items go together. Then tell why they are related.

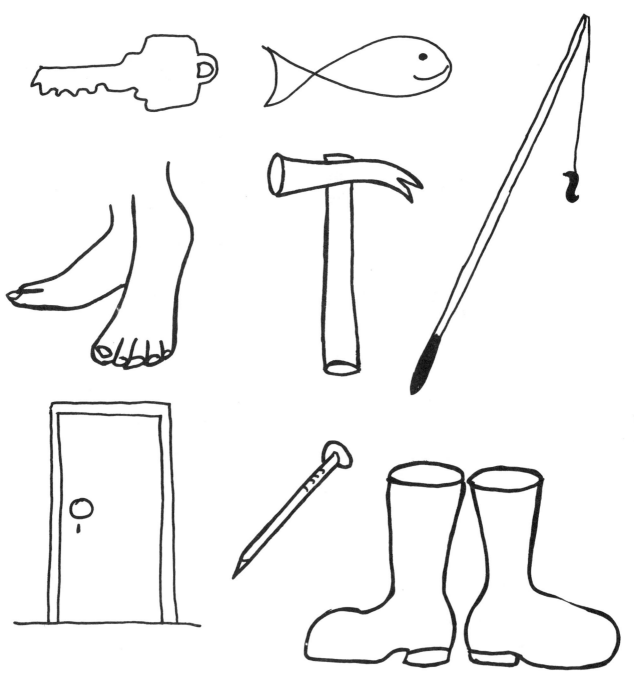

1–10 ASSOCIATION

Name _____

Directions: Draw a line to show which items go together. Then tell why they are related.

1–10 ASSOCIATION

Name _____

Directions: Draw a line to show which items go together. Then tell why they are related.

1–10 ASSOCIATION

Name _____

Directions: Draw a line to show which items go together. Then tell why they are related.

1–10 ASSOCIATION

63

Name _____

Directions: Draw a line to show which items go together. Then tell why they are related.

1–11 BUILDING CONCEPTS

Objective: The child will demonstrate understanding of the concepts "over," "under," "between," "on," and "around."

Rationale: These concepts are commonly called for in educational materials' directions. You will want to precede the worksheets with "real-life" experiences that involve following verbal directions, such as "put the book <u>on</u> the chair," "put your hand <u>over</u> your head," "walk <u>around</u> the desk," "put the paper <u>under</u> the book," or "stand <u>between</u> Jane and Tom."

Directions for Activity Sheets: For guided practice activities, show the child how to make a line "over" the flower, "under" the chair, and so on. For independent practice activities, give a direction such as "make a line over the cup" or "put an X on the cup."

Each activity sheet can be used several times so that you can change the directions with each successive use. For example, one time you might ask the child to "put an X on the cup," and then the next time you might say to "put a line under the cup."

Guided Practice

Independent Practice

1–11 BUILDING CONCEPTS (OVER/UNDER)

Name _____

Guided Practice

Independent Practice

1–11 BUILDING CONCEPTS (OVER/UNDER/ON)

Guided Practice

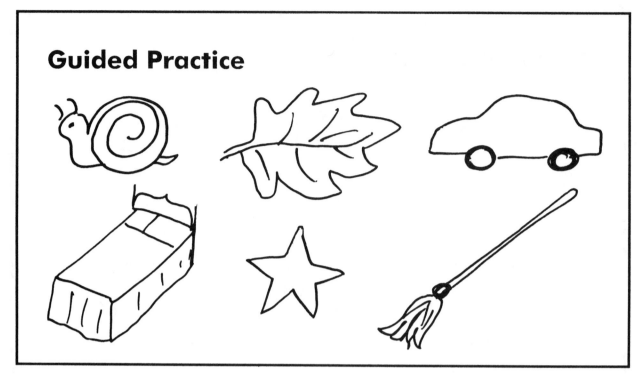

Independent Practice

1–11 BUILDING CONCEPTS (OVER/UNDER/ON) 68

Name _____

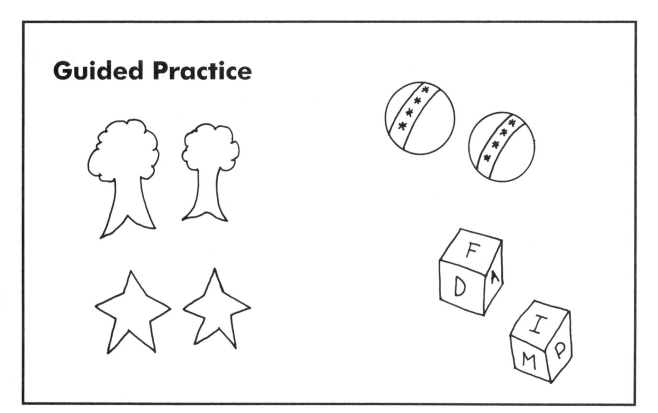

Guided Practice

Independent Practice

1–11 **BUILDING CONCEPTS (AROUND/BETWEEN)** 69

Guided Practice

c   c

Independent Practice

f f

UNIT 2

Beginning Academics

How to Teach Beginning Readers

In this chapter you will be introduced to a method for teaching reading that *works*. Children with poor memories have difficulty learning to read by the whole language approach, but they can learn to read by this method as presented here. The method has also proven beneficial with regular class children as well.

The method has two phases. First, you will teach the child a sound for each letter of the alphabet (except y); then, you will teach the child to blend the sounds together to get words.

2–1A SOUNDS LIST

Objective 1: The student will give the correct sound for each alphabet letter (except the letter y see page 77).

Rationale: The child is taught a single pictorial referent for each letter. We aim to teach this so well that when a child sees a letter, such as a, he or she will automatically see an apple in his or her mind's eye.

Directions: There are over 500,000 different words in the English language. To learn them all by pure memory would be an almost impossible job. The method being suggested here seeks to break words down into their component sounds (fewer than 50), thus simplifying the task. For children with memory deficits, this is often the difference between learning to read and not learning to read.

Teaching a sound for each letter is a process that usually takes about 20 *consecutive* days. The *longest* it has ever taken in my experience was about 60 days.

I have heard teachers complain that they get so tired of going over the same material daily, but, while it may be boring to the teachers, it usually is not boring to the child. If you sense that a child is bored, check him or her individually. If the child has learned all the sounds or has at least 22 of them, let the child become a helper (have the child go around the room while you are doing the lesson and make sure the other children are on task). The child will pick up the remaining sounds quickly, will feel less bored, and will enjoy greater self-esteem. Allow the child to wear a hat that says "Tutor" (made from a ring of construction paper).

If you check the child individually and he or she cannot give at least 22 of the sounds, show the child which ones he or she still needs to learn and tell the child that he or she can be a tutor as soon as the sounds are learned. To handle my own boredom, I remind myself that I will be extremely glad I did it because all my students will learn to read, and, in the long haul, this is the fastest and surest way to get those results.

During the initial phase, you and an aide (or parent or older child) can work with up to 35 children. You give the instruction at the board while the aide/helper circulates to see that the children are keeping up or are on task, drawing pictures and making the correct sounds. If someone has fallen behind, the helper sits with the child until he or she catches up or signals you to slow up a bit. By the second or third week, you may have a helper give the lesson while you circulate, which also relieves boredom but, in addition, allows the helper to become proficient in the method. Later, when the majority of the students have mastered the lesson, the helper can work with the few who need more time.

I have much better luck keeping children on task if I tell them before starting that they will get a cookie when we finish if they complete the worksheet.

I also send a letter to all parents inviting them to attend a session of "Sound Out." (Wait until the second week to send this letter so that you have established the routine with the students and having parents there will cause less disruption. If parents see what you are doing, they can do the same thing at home.)

Lesson Plan for Days 1–20:

Give each child a response sheet like the one on page 78. Say, "The things we will learn today will help you learn to read." Write an a on the board showing the children twice where it begins and how to form the letter. Give them time to trace over the letter on their sheet.

Next, using an overhead projector and a sheet that looks just like their worksheet, draw an apple in the box. Each child then draws an apple on his or her response sheet. Their apple may look as simple as a circle with a stem.

Say, "a says a." (Exaggerate the a sound as in apple. Be sure not to allow children to say, "a says apple.") Tell the children that apple is spelled a-p-p-l-e but the a says _____ (make the beginning sound again). Proceed through each letter by following these eight steps:

Step 1—Give the letter's name.

Step 2—Show how it is written.

Step 3—Have the children repeat, "The letter's name is _____."

Step 4—Say "The letter's sound is _____ as in _____ (give referent).

Step 5—The children repeat, "The letter's sound is _____."

Step 6—Draw the referent on the sheet (overhead).

Step 7—The children draw the referent on their sheets.

Step 8—Repeat, "The letter's sound is _____."

Do all 25 letters (no y) each day. For the first five days, you will need to take a break halfway through the lesson. Once the children have caught onto the system, you can complete the lesson in 30–35 minutes because they are able to draw faster.

One doubt teachers always express relates to whether young children can draw the pictures. Their drawings are not always clear to you, but after 20 days most children can give a sound for each letter. By requiring them to draw, you are calling their attention to the picture. It is a mistake to eliminate the drawings because then attention to the task is lost; you will end up spending more time teaching the objective.

Each day at the end of the lesson put up three to five words with the picture referents drawn below each word and help the children blend the sounds to get words. This helps the child see the purpose for learning the letter sounds. Suggested words include

Day 1	**Day 2**	**Day 3**	**Day 4**	**Day 5**
cat	up	ask	not	hat
pat	cup	cut	us	sat
tap	dog	hot	nap	sun

Day 6	**Day 7**	**Day 8**	**Day 9**	**Day 10**
rug	lap	at	let	met
bug	cap	in	leg	wet
bag	can	it	log	web

A word of caution: B̲ is not "buh"—it is only a pursing of the lips and a tiny poof of air. Likewise, C̲ is not "cu"— it makes the isolated k̲ sound.

The activity sheets on finding beginning consonants can be used on or after day 20.

© 1993 The Center for Applied Research in Education.

Date _____

Dear Parents,

Welcome to the new year. I am looking forward to getting to know you and your child. It is important that we keep in touch with each other often. We both want your child to have a successful, happy, and safe school year. If we work closely together as a team, I can almost guarantee things will go well. Please feel free to call me whenever you have a concern—any kind of concern—and I will make time for us to sit down face to face to talk.

I have found a method for teaching reading that really works. You are invited to come into the classroom and see how it works so that you can help your child at home. It is called "Sound Out," and we will be using it everyday for the next 20 days. If you and I work with your child in the same way, the learning will occur much faster. Please come visit our class on _____ at _____. If this time is not convenient, call me and we will reschedule for a day you can come.

Today's parents are very busy, I know, but if you could make time to read to your child for 10–15 minutes a day, it would help. If you do it just as you put the child to bed, you will find the child will go to sleep quicker. It also makes for some quality parent-child time.

Since we are aware that children sometimes forget to give notes to parents—and I really do want you to see "Sound Out"—please call or send me a note letting me know you are coming.

Sincerely,

_____

Teacher

2–1A LETTER TO PARENTS

Sounds List

a   (apple)   as in (apple)

j   (jar)

s   (snake)

b   (ball)

k   (kite)

t   (tack)

c   (car)

l   (lamp)

u   (up)

d   (door)

m   (moon)

v   (vase)

e   "The man fell off the edge"

n   (nose)

w   (water)

f   (fish)

o   (octopus)

x   says x

g   as in go

p   (pan)

y   The sound of y is taught as the child encounters it in reading

h   (house)

qu   (queen)

z   (zoo)

i   (itch)

r   (sounds like er as in her)

2–1A SOUNDS LIST

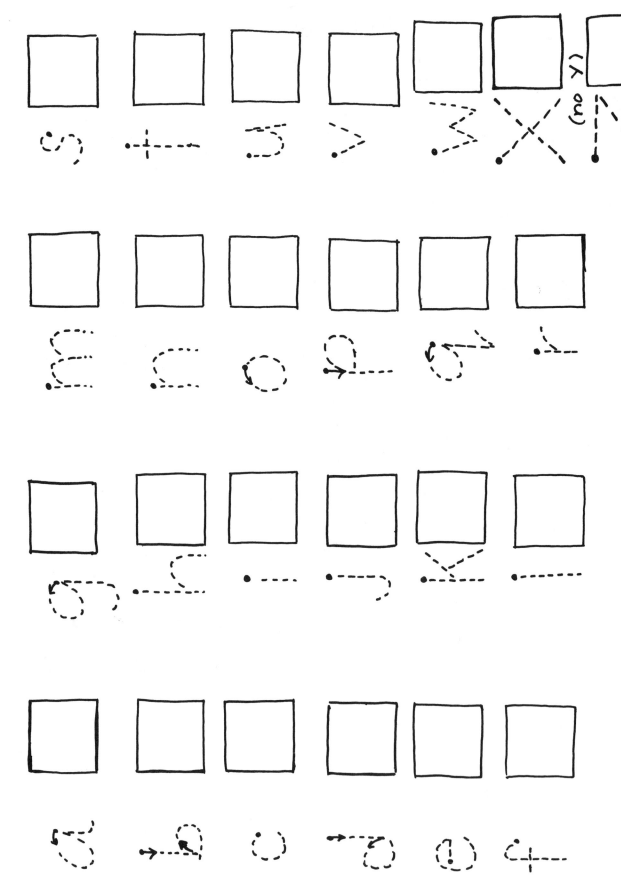

2–1A SOUNDS LIST—STUDENT RESPONSE SHEET

2–1B LETTERS AND SOUNDS

After the initial ten days of instruction, children enjoy laying out the alphabet letters (a–z) on the floor and then trying to match each letter with its referent picture. They may use the activity sheet from 2–1A that shows the matching pictures if they cannot remember the referent. You can make class sets from the 2–1B worksheets.

You may wish to use the letters and sounds for a border in your room or on the bulletin board. If so, enlarge and color them.

Lesson Plan for Days 11–30:

Objective 2: The child will blend words that have the vowel-consonant configuration (vc) and the consonant-vowel-consonant (cvc) configuration.

Rationale: Four out of every five words can be decoded. Learning to decode vc and cvc words is very exciting to children and whets their appetite to learn more.

Directions: After about ten days, you will want to begin to see the children for blending practice (ideally you will work with two to four children at a time). Present a word with its referents drawn below the letters. If a child can say the word, great! If no one can, then model and give help, carefully pointing to each letter as you make its sound. Be patient and model, model, model. It takes some children longer than others to catch on.

The children need help so they are not grunting sounds c.a.t. They must understand that the airflow over the vocal cords is steady (not interrupted). I tell children we are going to "sing" the sounds.

Words for initial blending practice may include

us	hug	mob	log	fat	map	full	jump	ask	ran
up	bug	bud	hog	sat	run	pull	camp	rap	gum
on	rug	dot	mop	dug	sun	flat	fast	hat	nap
am	tug	lot	top	job	bun	flag	last	plan	past
as	jug	rot	has	fun	hop	back	stop	off	not
at	had	fan	frog	soft	hot	box	sad	rag	hog
jam	bus	slap	mud	rat	mat	hut	but	glad	trap
and	pat	pup	mad	from	long	raft	spot	lamp	lap
dad	gun	can	got	pot	put	cat	cat	man	grab

You will want to show children how changing one letter in a word changes the word, for example; pat—pot—put; nap—lap—slap; cap— can—cat. As children master the a, o, u vowels, you can begin to intersperse i, e words into the practice session:

in	set	rib	best	let	fed	help	send	mess	belt
is	sit	men	gift	pet	bit	sled	lip	grin	red
it	tip	fit	tell	big	leg	slid	yes	kick	felt
if	sell	dip	clip	beg	milk	pen	hen	fix	rid
hit	hid	ten	yet	miss	pig	lick	lift	get	when
wet	fill	neck	bed	list	wig	spin	sick	did	left
net	web	fell	will	win	sip	met	nest	pet	leg

The i and e sounds are very hard for some children to discriminate. Remind them that i makes the sound heard in "itch" and e makes the sound heard in "edge."

Lesson Plan for Days 30–40:

Continue the previous activities with the students who have not mastered them, but add the next activity to the daily lesson plan.

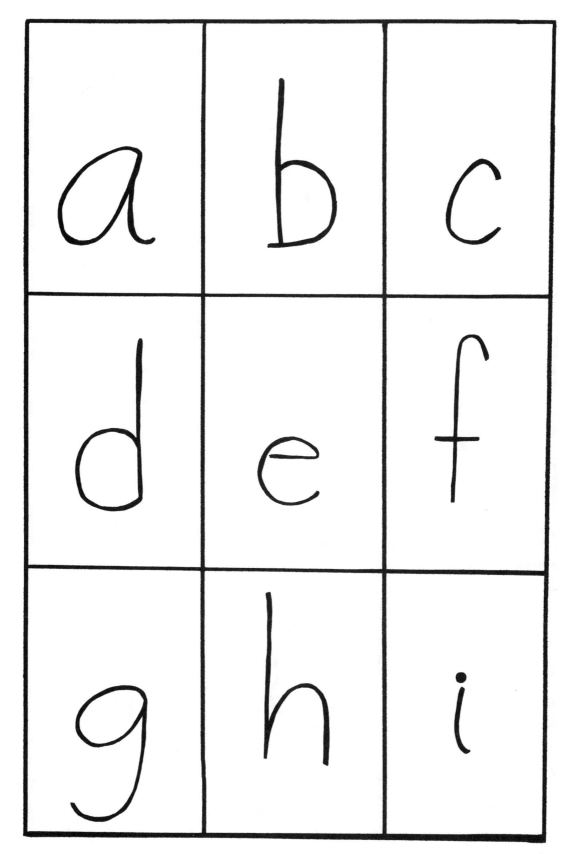

2–1B LETTERS AND SOUNDS—ALPHABET CARDS

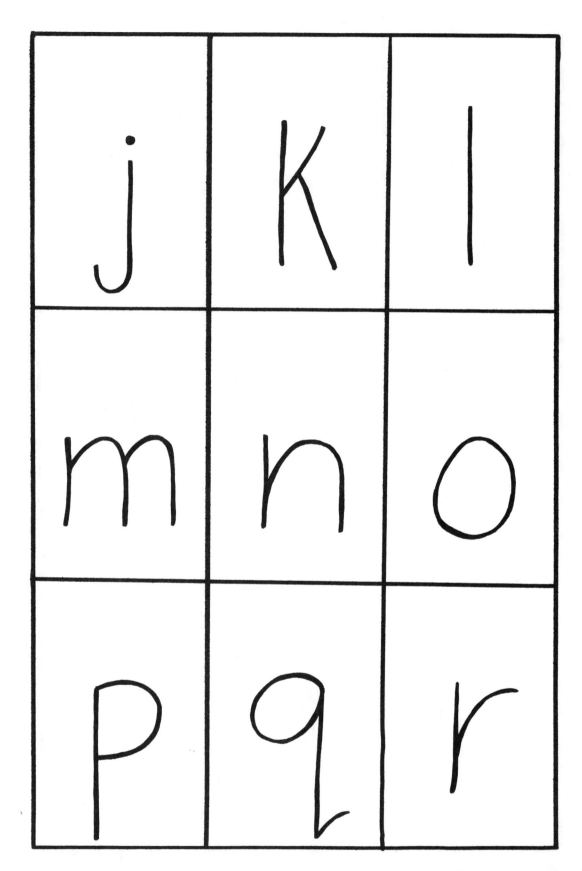

2–1B LETTERS AND SOUNDS—ALPHABET CARDS

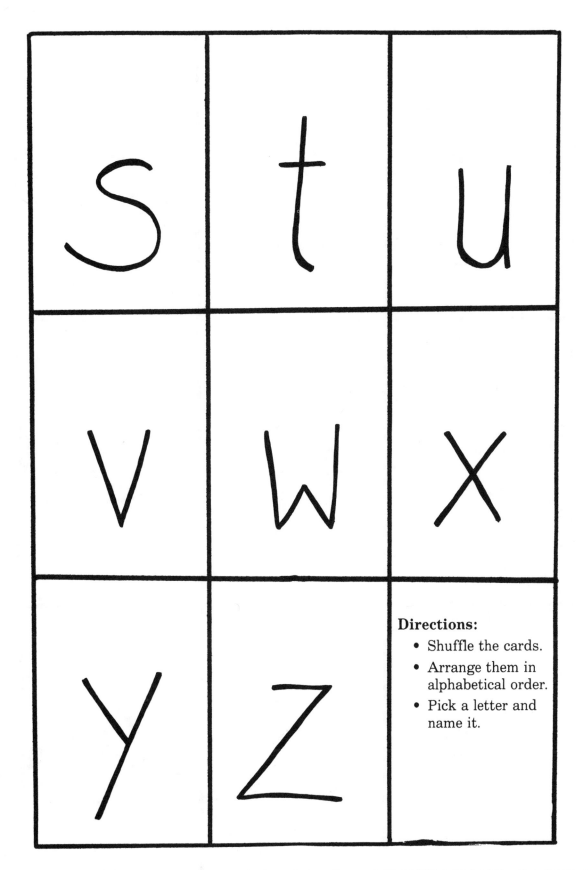

s	t	u
v	w	x
y	z	**Directions:** • Shuffle the cards. • Arrange them in alphabetical order. • Pick a letter and name it.

2–1B LETTERS AND SOUNDS—ALPHABET CARDS

2–1B LETTERS AND SOUNDS—SOUNDS CARDS 84

2–1B LETTERS AND SOUNDS—SOUNDS CARDS 85

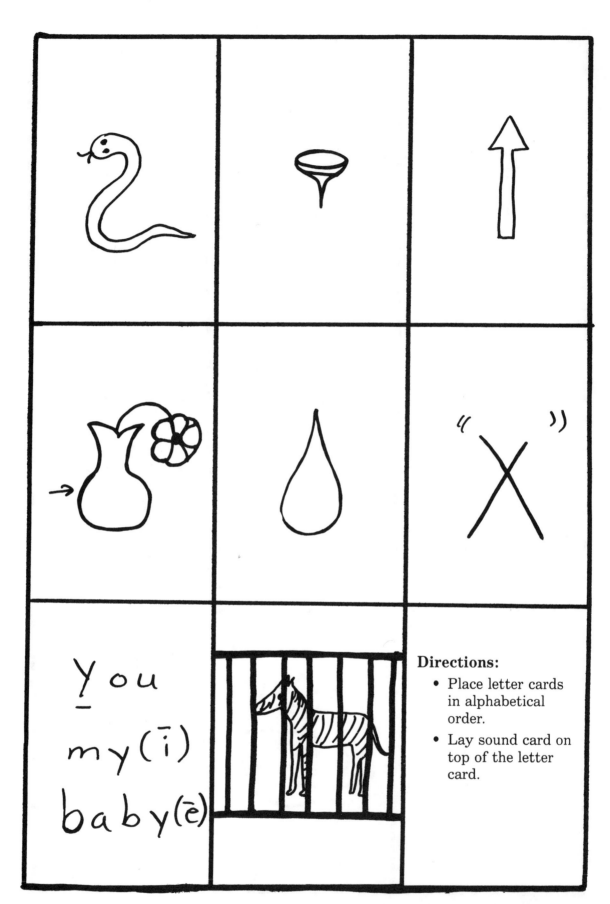

y̲ou

my (ī)

baby (ē)

Directions:
- Place letter cards in alphabetical order.
- Lay sound card on top of the letter card.

2–1B LETTERS AND SOUNDS—SOUNDS CARDS   86

2-1C VOWEL SOUNDS

The materials found in this section are designed to help you teach children about vowel sounds. Materials for bulletin board display are included.

Objective 3: The student will be able to identify the vowels.

Rationale: Once the student can decode short vowel words, we must teach the child to recognize vowels so that he or she will be able to decode words that have the long vowel sound.

Directions: You can introduce this lesson by saying, "Children are either boys or girls. If you are not a boy, you must be a girl. Likewise, there are two kinds of letters—vowels and consonants. The vowels are a, e, i, o, u, and sometimes y and w. If a letter is not a vowel, then it must be a consonant.

Each day for the next ten days, give the children practice locating the vowels in words. At this point it is not important for the child to be able to read the word, but we must teach him or her to note whether the word has more than one vowel.

Put a list of ten words on the board daily. Have the children repeat "The vowels are a, e, i, o, u, and sometimes y and w." Ask a student to come up and put a v under each vowel in the word:

cup   At first you may need to write the vowels on the
v   board and prompt the student by asking, "Is
             there an a in the word? How about an e? i? o? u?
later   y? w?"
v v

Each day give the child a list of five to ten words so he or she can practice locating the vowels. Continue to give each child this practice until the skill is mastered.

At this point you will want to expand your Vowel Bulletin Board so it looks like this:

At some point, children are introduced to a reader. The reader used is usually determined by your school district. At first, you will need to go very slowly. Learning to read is much like a train leaving the station—at first it moves slowly, but as it moves on it gains speed. In the beginning, encourage the children to work for accuracy. Speed will come as frequently encountered words reach the automatic level.

Basal readers build sight vocabularies one word at a time. They attempt to teach each word to mastery. The stories are stilted because of the limited vocabulary. The emphasis is on acquiring reading skill, and the hope is that, at some time in the future, the child will learn to love to read.

The philosophy of the whole language approach is different. The child listens to a story for enjoyment; then he or she goes over and over the story until the vocabulary is stuck in his or her head. Proponents of this approach say the student will gradually pick up basic skills.

The *average* child will learn to read no matter how reading is taught, but children who are not reading by the end of grade 1 or who have poor memories will need a strong phonics approach. The skills in this book will help you meet those children's needs.

If you have no district-mandated text, the *Multiple Skills* series published by Barnell-Loft (available by writing to the publisher at 958 Church Street, Baldwin, New York 11510) is excellent. Since it is not a new program, you might find it if you look around your school or ask around your district. You will need Picture Level, Introductory Level, Preparatory Level, and the A Level in grade 1. Later you can add further levels as they are needed.

The *Multiple Skills* series is carefully developed. As new words are introduced, a concerted effort is made to use them again and again in the next few pages. Therefore, it is important for a child to move from the front of the book forward (no skipping around). Skills covered involve comprehension, visual awareness, inferential thinking, scanning for information, and vocabulary development.

When you begin the Picture Level, start by asking the child to tell you what is happening in the picture. Then the child reads the words and answers the questions. If you then ask the child to write a sentence about the story, he or she will get additional exposure to the words. It is also helpful to isolate two or three words each day and ask the child to tell you which letters he or she can hear. This reinforces the skills you have taught and draws attention to letters that cannot be heard, such as the silent e in home.

As you go along, be alert for the introduction of the two-vowel rule. The rhyme "when two vowels go walking, the first one does the talking" means nothing to many children. What does work is to tell them about "the bully." For example, r.a.n. spells ran, but if you add another vowel, as in r.a.i.n., the i (the bully) reaches over and tells the a, "You had better say your name. Don't you say a as in apple. Don't you dare! You say a (with your voice make the long a sound)." At first the child will need daily practice in applying this rule.

Objective 4:   When shown words with the cvvc and cvcv configuration, the child will orally decode them.

Rationale: The addition of this rule to the child's knowledge will dramatically expand the number of words a child can read.

Lesson Plan for Days 40–60:

Give children daily exposure to decoding words that have two vowels in them.

Directions: Some words you can use to illustrate the two-vowel rule are given here. Point to the e and say "The e is the bully. The e doesn't make a sound but tells the first vowel to say its name."

can—cane
us—use
hop—hope
cap—cape
hat—hate
rob—robe
kit—kite
fed—feed
bed—bead
slid—slide
pin—pine
met—meat

rid—ride
tub—tube
cut—cute
men—mean
set—seat
dim—dime
cot—coat
red—read
rip—ripe
bit—bite
got—goat

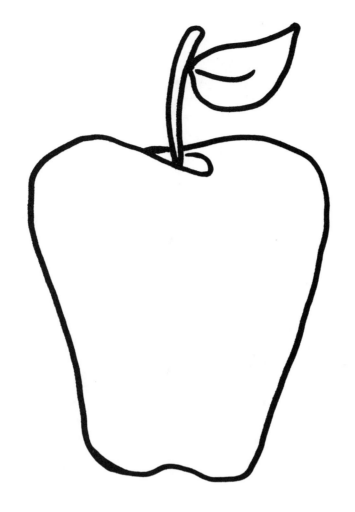

a   apple

2–1C VOWEL SOUNDS—VOWEL BULLETIN BOARD

e   edge

2–1C VOWEL SOUNDS—VOWEL BULLETIN BOARD

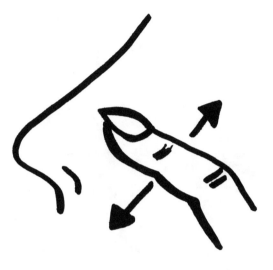

i   <u>i</u>tch

2–1C VOWEL SOUNDS—VOWEL BULLETIN BOARD

O octopus

2–1C VOWEL SOUNDS—VOWEL BULLETIN BOARD

u up

2–1C VOWEL SOUNDS—VOWEL BULLETIN BOARD

2–1D UNBLENDING WORDS

Lesson Plan for Days 61–80:

Objective 5: The child will be able to unblend (spell) words with the vc, cvc, and cvcc configurations.

Rationale: By this point the children are able to read (blend sounds together to get a word). Now we introduce the reverse process (unblending has the child break a word down into its component parts). This is the beginning of spelling. If children master this objective, they will be able to produce written work that is phonetically correct and, therefore, readable. They will be able to communicate in writing.

Directions: For the next 20 days, you will need to give the children practice in listening to a word and then trying to figure out how it is spelled (unblending). The easiest way to do this is to provide the children with small chalkboards to use at their desks (they can bring an old sock for an eraser). If chalkboards are not available, the activity can be done on paper. The advantage of the chalkboard is twofold: the children like them and it saves you time. You can have the children turn the chalkboards toward you so that from the front of the room, you can quickly check each child's work.

Each day choose a list of eight words. On the first day, start with vc words, such as <u>up</u>, <u>at</u>, <u>in</u>, <u>us</u>, <u>is</u>, <u>it</u>, <u>as</u>, and <u>an</u>. Tell the child to write two spaces on the board/paper like this:

_____   _____

(vowel)   (consonant)

Tell the children that you are going to say a two-letter word. They are going to repeat the word slowly out loud, listening to see if they can hear the two sounds. Point out that the first sound will be a vowel and that the children will write the vowel in the first space. Point out that the second letter is a consonant and that the children will write it in the second space.

After you give the word and they write it or try to, put the answer on the board. Demonstrate how you can hear each sound by saying the word and overexaggerating each sound.

On the next day, give half of the words from the previous lesson but add about four using the cvc configuration. Before saying each word, write on the board what they are looking for (vc or cvc).

Continue daily practice. About the 15th day, begin adding words with the cvcc configuration, such as fast or jump.

By the 20th day, the majority of your class will be able to meet this objective. You (parents or aides can do this if they have been present daily because they know the system) will need to continue to work with the few students who are lagging on the five objectives. You may find this is easier to do if you change the seating so those who are behind sit near you (sometimes this won't work because the students can't get along with each other, but if they can, it will make your life easier).

The activity sheets given can be used for seatwork (after day 80). You may have to do some input so the youngsters know what they are seeing.

Answers:

hat, man, sun, top	cat, gum, bag, pot
bus, web, cup, dog	gun, rip, jug, nut
cap, pin, bed, log	jam (or jar), mop, ten, box
pig, rug, bat, bug	cot, net, can, fan

club, drum, flag, trap
sled, plug, crab, frog

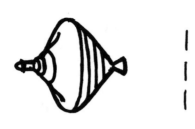

2–1D UNBLENDING WORDS

Name _____

2–1D UNBLENDING WORDS

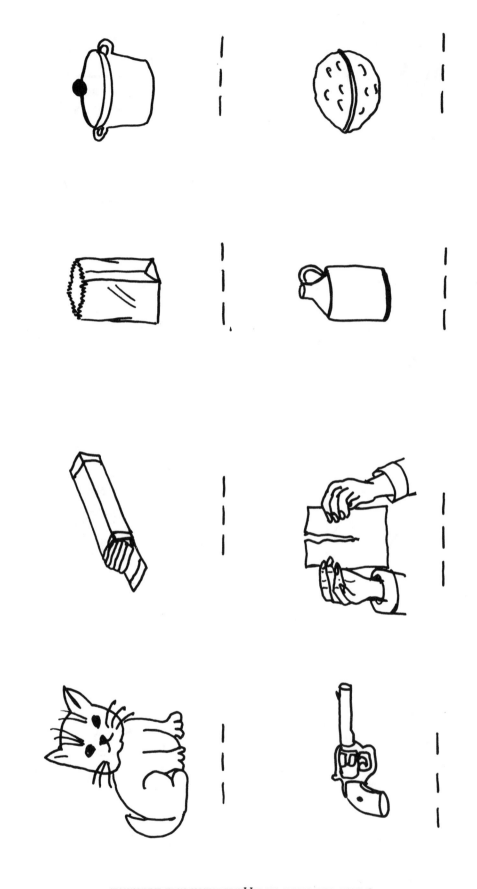

2–1D UNBLENDING WORDS

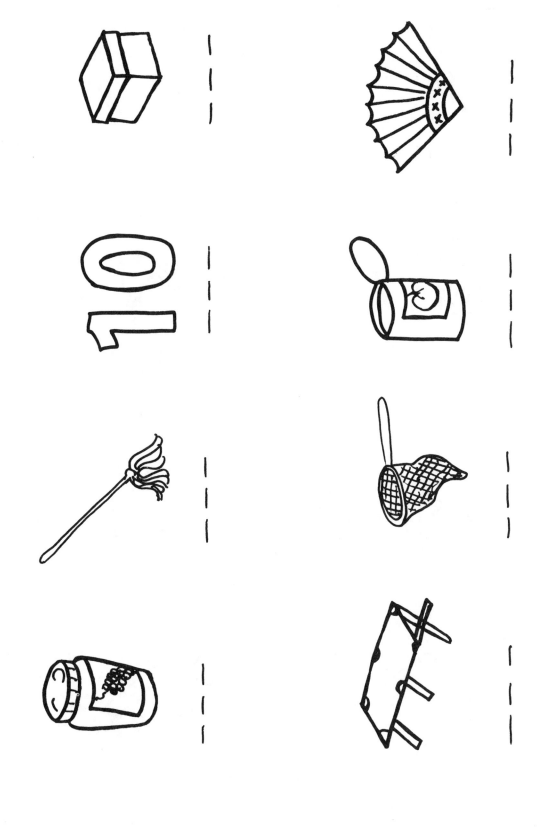

Name

2–1D UNBLENDING WORDS

102

2–2 SPECIAL COMBINATIONS AND TEACHER RESOURCE WORD LISTS

Objective: The student will be able to decode one-syllable words that contain special combinations.

Rationale: The child will begin to encounter what I refer to as "special combinations." You will find a chart of these in Unit Three labeled "Student Reminder for Decoding." You will want to familiarize yourself thoroughly with these combinations so you are alert to their introduction in the reading text that you are using. As they are introduced, you will need to spend a little time daily talking about them and having students decode words that use them.

Directions: Usually sh, th, and ch are the first combinations that are introduced. I tell the children that when s gets next to h, they become stuck together just like peanut butter sticks to bread and they cannot be separated. They take on a whole new sound—sounding like the noise you make when you tell someone to be quiet. Likewise, th and ch have their own sounds.

Research has told us that most children have to be told something 90 times before they know it! You can shorten that number of needed number of exposures if you will *make a big deal of each combination as you introduce it* and *give daily practice using the combination*. The Teacher Resource Word Lists will help you develop your daily exposure to each new combination.

sh

ch

th

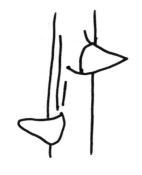

__orn

__ell

__in

__ree

di__

mat__

2–2 SPECIAL COMBINATIONS—TEACHING THREE COMMON CONSONANT BLENDS

Name _____

sh

ch

th

__ __ur__ __

__ __irt

bru__ __

pa__ __

__ __ain

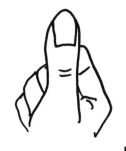

__ __umb

2–2 SPECIAL COMBINATIONS—TEACHING
THREE COMMON CONSONANT BLENDS

Teacher Resource Word Lists
of Special Combinations

sh easy (short vowel)

shut	ship	shop
shed	shell	shock
dish	wish	fish
fresh	rush	brush
crush	gush	push
trash	cash	mash
crash	sash	rash

sh (long vowel)

shape	shade	shame
shake	sheep	shore
shine	shone	leash

sh (with two or more combinations)

sh ar p	sh oo t	sh ou t
sh ow	sh or t	sh ow er

th easy (short vowel)

this	that	them
then	think	thank
tenth	path	bath
cloth	moth	math

th (long vowel)

three	these
teeth	those

th (more than one combination)

th r ow	th ir d	th ir st
th or n	th ing	

ch (short vowel)

chin	chip	chop
chest	check	chick
catch	much	such

ch (long vowel)

chair	chase	chose
cheap	cheek	cheese
cheer	bench	each
reach	beach	teach
peach	lunch	bunch

© 1993 The Center for Applied Research in Education.

Teacher Resource Word Lists
of Special Combinations (continued)

ch (more than one combination)

ch ei f	ch an ce	ch ar ge
ch ur ch	p er ch	p or ch

wa as in "water"

was	wash	walk
watch	want	water

oo as in "too"

soon	tool	pool
cool	food	stool
school	smooth	boot
roof	hoof	room
moon	broom	spoon
scoop	tooth	shoot
booth	troop	

ing

sing	king	ring
bring	sting	wing
swing	thing	string
spring	finger	

ow as "ou" (ouch)

now	how	cow
brown	down	town
crown	crowd	drown

ow as "o" (w is acting as a vowel)

show	slow	grow
flow	bowl	below
follow	blow	own
grown	sown	window

ow as "ou" (in combination with other elements)

t ow er	p ow er	p ow der
ch ow der	fl ow er	

2–2 TEACHER RESOURCE WORD LISTS (continued)

Teacher Resource Word Lists
of Special Combinations (continued)

ew (oo) as in "new"

flew	new	blew
stew	crew	chew
grew	threw	

ou as in "loud"

round	sound	hound
pound	cloud	proud
ground	found	mouse
house	our	

ou (with other combinations)

s ou th	m ou th	ou ch

ar as in "hard"

bar	car	jar
far	farm	star
bark	dark	carve
hard	card	park
part	smart	arm
art	yard	

wr (w is silent)

write	wreck	wrist
wrong	wrote	wrap

kn (k is silent)

knee	knife	knew
knot	knock	know

er as "r"

her	after	enter
later	offer	winter

ir as "r"

bird	girl	first
shirt	birth	dirt

© 1993 The Center for Applied Research in Education.

2–2 TEACHER RESOURCE WORD LISTS (continued)

Teacher Resource Word Lists
of Special Combinations (continued)

ur as "r"

burn	turn	hurt
burst	during	curve

or

for	north	born
storm	porch	order

aw as in "saw"

jaw	paw	raw
draw	crawl	

au as in "because"

haul	auto	fault
daughter	caught	

oi as in "oil"

boil	soil	point
join	coin	foil
hoist	moist	

oy as in "boy"

toy	joy	enjoy
royal		

2–2 TEACHER RESOURCE WORD LISTS (continued)

2–3 BEGINNING WORD LIST

Around the end of the third month of school, you will want to make a notebook or folder for each child to keep in his or her desk. Make copies of the Beginning Word List to go in the folder. Also make a copy of the list to go home with the child. If you laminate the lists, they will last longer. It is also a good idea to put the child's name on the back so it can be returned if lost.

Objective 1: The child will recognize the words on the list and will use the list when writing.

Rationale: We want children to be self-reliant. This list will help do that. We want to minimize the demands on teacher time. The children can check spelling using the list rather than bother you or an aide. Last, if you can prevent misspelling, you can speed up the internalization of the correct spelling of the words.

Directions: On the first day you give out the list, you will need to practice how to use it. Say a word. Ask what letters they can hear. Write those letters on the board. Then have them find the word on the list. If the word on the board needs correction, fix it. You will need to do the activity for several days to be sure the children know how to use the list. Thereafter, if a child asks how to spell a word that is on the list, you simply remind him or her gently to check his or her list.

Objective 2: The student will be able to spell the words from the list correctly.

Rationale: We want to help children learn to spell the words they encounter frequently. The words on the list are ones that appear again and again in readers at this level. The more exposures a child has to a word, the more likely he or she is to remember it. By using words from this list for weekly spelling, you are increasing the likelihood that the child will learn to read and spell the words.

Date _____

Dear _____,

We have made a good beginning. Now I would like to enlist your help again. We want _____ to become a proficient speller. Therefore, you will find a list of words that we will be concentrating on this year.

There are many ways parents can help the child learn these words. First, you may want to put the words on index cards—one word on each side. Have the child say the words as you flash them to him or her. If _____ is not able to tell you a given word, give the word's name to _____. Then ask, "Which letters in the word can you hear?"

Once _____ can recognize all the words, you might want to choose three words to learn to spell. The next night, go over the three words again and add another word. Each night you review the words done the day before and add a new word. When you get up to 30 words, begin giving them in random order. When you get up to 50, you can drop those that are never missed.

Some sort of SMALL REWARD CAN MAKE HOMEWORK MORE PLEAS-ANT—a treat to eat or a dime to spend at the store. You do not want to give more because as children grow up, you may need to increase the reward to get their effort, and if you began big, there is no room to move.

Please send me a note once a week letting me know which words you are working on. Thank you!

_____
Teacher

2–3 LETTER TO PARENTS

Beginning Word List

all	are	away
and	at	ask
big	blue	ball
boy	but	bed
book	by	be
black	brown	back
can	call	could
cat	car	came
come	cut	
do	day	done
did	dog	don't
does	down	
eat	each	every

2–3 BEGINNING WORD LIST—NOTEBOOK MATERIALS

Beginning Word List (continued)

fall	food	for
far	from	fun
find	found	friend
	father	

get	gave	green
girl	give	grow
go	good	goes
going		

had	him	house
has	his	home
hat	her	how
hot	have	help
he	here	happy

is	if	in	it

jump	just

2–3 BEGINNING WORD LIST—NOTEBOOK MATERIALS (continued)

Beginning Word List (continued)

let	like	little
long	look	love

may	made	make
man	me	mother
much	my	must

no	not	new	now

one	of	old
on	out	over
off	orange	our

play	put	pull

ran	read	ride
run	red	

said	sat	sing
see	saw	sleep
some	so	soon
stop	school	stay

2–3 BEGINNING WORD LIST—NOTEBOOK MATERIALS (continued)

Beginning Word List (continued)

the	this	that
to	two	too
toy	take	tell
them	there	time
thing	told	tree
up	us	use
very		
who	what	where
why	when	we
went	want	will
with	walk	water
were	would	white
yes	you	your
	yellow	

2–3 BEGINNING WORD LIST—NOTEBOOK MATERIALS (continued)

2–4 RHYMING WORDS AND WORD FAMILIES

Objective: The student will use his or her knowledge of rhyming words to construct word families. When given a word, the child will make new words and spell them simply by changing the first letter of the given word.

Rationale: Learning this skill enhances the child's ability to spell because he or she realizes that every word is not a new word. For instance, if a child learns to spell <u>night</u> by changing the first letter, he or she can also spell many more words—light, fight, might, tight, sight, right.

In the early grades, teachers need to remind children of this premise often. If the child asks, "How do you spell cook?" have the child try to think of a word in the same family. Say, "You can spell <u>look</u>. <u>Cook</u> is just like <u>look</u> except for the first letter." Print the words <u>look</u>, <u>cook</u>, and <u>book</u> on the chalkboard so the child can see the similarity.

Directions for Activity Sheets: Have the child name all the words and then spell the rhyming words.

Answers:
purse—nurse, fish—dish, book—hook, nest—vest
bug—rug, cube—tube, tag—bag, coat—boat
pan—man, block—clock, cone—bone, fire—tire
star—car, dog—log, bell—well, hose—rose
pie—tie, horn—corn, bat—cat, wall—ball

Name _____

Directions: Name all the words. Spell the rhyming word.

nest

book

fish

purse

_ _ _ _

_ _ _ _

_ _ _ _

_ _ _ _

2–4 RHYMING WORDS/WORD FAMILIES

Name _____

Directions: Name all the words. Spell the rhyming word.

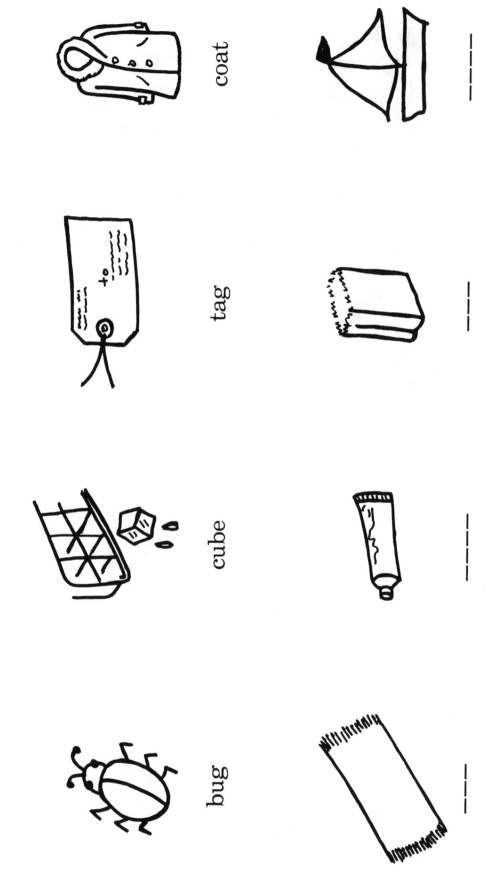

bug   cube   tag   coat

_ _ _   _ _ _   _ _ _   _ _ _

2–4 RHYMING WORDS/WORD FAMILIES

Name _____

Directions: Name all the words. Spell the rhyming word.

fire

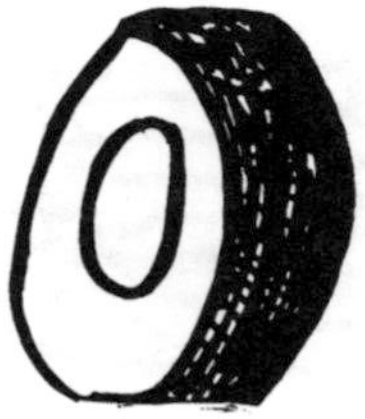

cone

block

pan

_ _ _ _

_ _ _ _

_ _ _ _

_ _ _ _

2–4 RHYMING WORDS/WORD FAMILIES

Name _____

Directions: Name all the words. Spell the rhyming word.

 hose

 bell

 dog

star

_ _ _ _

well
_ _ _

log
_ _ _

_ _ _

120

2-4 RHYMING WORDS/WORD FAMILIES

Name

Directions: Name all the words. Spell the rhyming word.

wall

bat

horn

pie

_ _ _

_ _ _

_ _ _

_ _ _

2–4 **RHYMING WORDS/WORD FAMILIES**

121

2–5 TURNING WORDS INTO MENTAL IMAGES

Objective: The student will read a short passage and demonstrate that he or she has converted the words into mental images by drawing a picture of what he or she read.

Rationale: Sometimes beginning readers get so caught up in the act of decoding that they forget to think about what they read. We want to make multiple opportunities in the lower grades for them to draw a picture to go with the story or to act out a part of the story or to paraphrase what they read so that we are sure they are comprehending the material. The questions found in the *Multiple Skills* series are helpful because they allow you to assess quickly whether the child understood what he or she read.

Directions for Activity Sheets: These worksheets assess comprehension. Have the child draw a picture to show what each sentence means.

The house sat at the top of a tall hill.	A big dog ran after the cat.
Jim had to put out the trash.	The girl wore a blue dress.

2–5 TURNING WORDS INTO MENTAL IMAGES

Name _____

The box is on the bed.	I cut my hand. Mother put something on it.
There are two girls playing under the tree.	On a leaf was a red bug with black spots on its back.

Name _____

She has a slide, three swings, and a sandbox in her yard.	Father made a snowman. Our cat sat on its head.
Mother is reading a story to me.	He put too much food in his mouth.

2–5 TURNING WORDS INTO MENTAL IMAGES 125

Name _____

The car has a flat tire.	My book fell on the floor.
I set two plates and two cups on the tray.	She had picked a bunch of flowers.

2–5 TURNING WORDS INTO MENTAL IMAGES

Name _____

Dad got a saw and cut down the tree.	Our dog likes to play with her toy ball.
Tom went to the store on his bike.	I saw two cars. One was black and one was white.

2–5 TURNING WORDS INTO MENTAL IMAGES

| We saw her fall down the steps. | My friend got a new hat. |
| I went to sleep on the rug by the T.V. | The little boy gave me his toy. |

2–5 TURNING WORDS INTO MENTAL IMAGES   128

Name _____

Three cats are on the porch.	I helped wash dishes.
We lined up for lunch.	It was raining very hard.

2–5 TURNING WORDS INTO MENTAL IMAGES

2-6 BUILDING SENTENCES

Objective 1: The student will demonstrate that he or she can construct longer and more interesting sentences—ones that contain a noun, a verb, and a phrase.

Rationale: Young children need to be encouraged to write more interesting sentences. Time needs to be spent helping them begin sentences with some other word than "I." Being young, they relate to the world from the "I" position. We need to encourage them to start sentences with other people, such as Mother, Father, we, the children, and so on, or with names of things, such as "The cat," "The ball," "The swing," and so on.

Directions for Activity Sheets: The worksheets in this section encourage the children to write interesting sentences by forcing them to choose from the words provided.

Objective 2: The student will be able to answer two questions:

> "How do we begin a sentence?" (*Answer:* with a capital letter)
>
> "How do we end a sentence?" (*Answer:* with a period or question mark or exclamation point)

Rationale: At this level we are trying to make the child aware of these simple mechanics. As the worksheets are completed, many reminders need to be given.

Putting a capital letter at the beginning and terminal punctuation at the end of sentences is usually not habitually done until well into the third year of school. Keep reminding!

Name _____

1. _____
   _____

2. _____
   _____

3. _____
   _____

Subject	Predicate	Phrase
The children	is playing	over the wall.
The girl	are eating	with her ball
	is looking	a snack.

2–6 BUILDING SENTENCES

1. _____

2. _____

3. _____

Subject	Predicate	Phrase
The children	is sleeping	a book.
A boy	are playing	in the sun.
	is getting	in the sand.

2–6 BUILDING SENTENCES

1. _____

2. _____

3. _____

Subject	Predicate	Phrase
A cat	are playing	on his sweater.
The boy	is putting	a game.
Two children	is playing	with a ball.

2–6 BUILDING SENTENCES

1. _____
_____

2. _____
_____

3. _____
_____

Subject
The girl
Two children
The boy

Predicate
is helping
are walking
has

Phrase
in the hall.
his dad.
two dogs.

2–6 BUILDING SENTENCES

1. _____
   _____

2. _____
   _____

3. _____
   _____

Subject	Predicate	Phrase
The boy	is building	a nest.
The bird	is eating	a bird house.
Mother	is making	ice cream.

2–6 BUILDING SENTENCES

135

1.

2.

3.

Subject
I
The girl

Predicate
can see
is washing
is cooking

Phrase
her dog.
three fish.
a fish.

2–6 BUILDING SENTENCES

Name _____

1. _____
   _____

2. _____
   _____

3. _____
   _____

Subject	Predicate	Phrase
Two children	is putting	very fast.
The girl	are running	ball today.
	is playing	on her skates.

2–6 BUILDING SENTENCES

1. _____
   _____

2. _____
   _____

3. _____
   _____

Subject	Predicate	Phrase
Two mice	are eating	here.
The man	sees	some cheese.
The girl	is coming	three birds.

2–6 BUILDING SENTENCES

2–7 ALPHABETIZING

Objective: The student will alphabetize a list of six words by the first letter.

Rationale: This is a commonly taught first-grade skill. It is the first step in preparation for filing or dictionary use.

Directions: The activity sheets in this segment use words from the Beginning Word List.

To introduce the children to the skill, give them an alphabet strip from which to work. Have them circle the first letter of each word. Explain that that is the letter they are to look at. Ask, "Do I have a word that begins with a?" If so, write it down. "Do I have a word that starts with b?" If so, write it down. Continue to model the skill by going through each letter. Sometimes a child will need to cross off each letter on his or her strip to keep his or her place.

Teach the child to proofread his or her work. At the end of an exercise, have the child say the alphabet and touch the first letter of each entry.

a b c d e f g h i j k l m n o p q r s t u v w x y z

a b __ __ e f __ i __ __ __ m __ __

q r s __ __ __ w x __ __

a __ c __ j __ l __ s __ u __

d __ f __ m __ o __ w __ z

g __ i __ p __ r

a __ __ d __ __ g __ j __ m __ p

q __ __ t __ __ w __ z

2-7 ALPHABETIZING

Name _____

a b c d e f g h i j k l m n o p q r s t u v w x y z

Directions: • Circle the first letter of each word.
           • Alphabetize.   • Name the words.

big	1. _____
eat	2. _____
did	3. _____
and	4. _____
can	5. _____
for	6. _____

had	1. _____
just	2. _____
did	3. _____
get	4. _____
like	5. _____
make	6. _____

2–7 ALPHABETIZING

a b c d e f g h i j k l m n o p q r s t u v w x y z

Directions: • Circle the first letter of each word.
             • Alphabetize.   •Name the words.

big	1. _____
look	2. _____
ask	3. _____
not	4. _____
cat	5. _____
good	6. _____

me	1. _____
put	2. _____
black	3. _____
see	4. _____
girl	5. _____
two	6. _____

2–7 ALPHABETIZING

142

Name _____

a b c d e f g h i j k l m n o p q r s t u v w x y z

Directions: • Circle the first letter of each word.
• Alphabetize. • Name the words.

man	1. _____
red	2. _____
we	3. _____
saw	4. _____
day	5. _____
over	6. _____

when	1. _____
in	2. _____
cut	3. _____
must	4. _____
up	5. _____
every	6. _____

2–7 ALPHABETIZING

a b c d e f g h i j k l m n o p q r s t u v w x y z

Directions: • Circle the first letter of each word.
• Alphabetize. •Name the words.

when	1. _____
you	2. _____
time	3. _____
play	4. _____
on	5. _____
read	6. _____

hot	1. _____
us	2. _____
old	3. _____
stop	4. _____
it	5. _____
from	6. _____

2–7 ALPHABETIZING

2–8 STORY PROBLEMS

Objective: The child will be able to solve story problems in math using visual helps.

Rationale: Solving story problems is one area that gives children trouble. It is basically a reading/conceptual skill; therefore, it has been included in this book. Solving story problems requires that the child convert words into mental images.

Directions for Activity Sheets: In this section are problems and pictures to help the child solve the problem using concrete manipulative tools. After reading the problem, the child will cut and paste pictures to demonstrate his or her understanding of the process involved.

Extension: In first grade there is a need for children to play store. It has come to my attention, however, that children do not understand the process of buying; they do not understand that if they pay 8 cents for a ball and hand the clerk a dime, the change will be 2 cents.

Assemble a group of items. Upon initiating this concept, mark the prices under 10 cents and work with pennies. You play the part of clerk so you can model the reasoning that is involved in the transaction. You can also model how a clerk acts (prevocational training). It might sound like this:

As the child brings the item he or she selected to you, you say, "Good morning, Miss (or Mr.) _____. That will be 8 cents, please." At first, the child can just hand you the 8 pennies. Then you say, "Thank you. Have a nice day." Bag the items and wave goodbye.

After a little practice, give the child a dime (real money really embellishes the lesson). Go through a similar greeting, but as the child hands you the dime, say, "How many pennies is this worth?" Draw 10 marks on the board and say, "(Sarah) owes me 8 cents. I will take the 8 cents out of the dime. Remember that the dime is worth 10 pennies." Then you cross out marks saying, "You owe me 1, 2, 3, 4, 5, 6, 7, 8 cents. How many marks are left? That is your change." Hand the child the bag and say, "This was 8 cents (touching the bag)."

Hand the child the penny, touch the bag, and say, "8 + 1 is 9." Put another penny in her hand and say, "10." On the board, draw the bag and write "8" on it. Draw the pennies and write "1" on them, and touching the numbers, say, "8 + 1 + 1 makes 8, 9, 10."

After the children understand amounts to 10, go on to making change from a quarter. When they show readi-

145

ness, you can have them buy two items (adding) and then make change from the quarter. Later, have the children be the clerk.

Since so many story problems involve money and counting, playing store is time well spent.

Name _____

1. Put _____ fish in the bowl.
2. Now add _____ more fish.
3. How many fish in all?

    _____

2–8 STORY PROBLEMS (CUT AND PASTE ACTIVITY)

Guided Practice

- Ask five girls to come to the front of the room. Then ask three boys to come up.
- Ask the class:
  "How many children in all?"
  (Count together.)
- "How many more girls than boys?"
  (Have them pair off.)
- Do the activity again, using different numbers of children.

Check Understanding

- There are _____ girls.
- There are _____ boys.
- "How many children in all?" _____
- "How many more _____ than _____?"
  Show solution here or on the back (Cut and paste.)

© 1993 The Center for Applied Research in Education.

Candy costs ___ each.

You want ___ candies.

They will cost ___.

(Show solution on the back.)

On a card there are ___ buttons.

You use ___.

How many are left? ___

(Show solution on the back.)

2–8 STORY PROBLEMS—SET I (CUT AND PASTE ACTIVITY)

You need ___ buttons.

They come on a card.

There are ___ buttons
on each card.

How many cards will you
need to buy? ___

(Show solution on the back.)

___ balls.

___ are red.

How many are not red?

(Show solution on the back.)

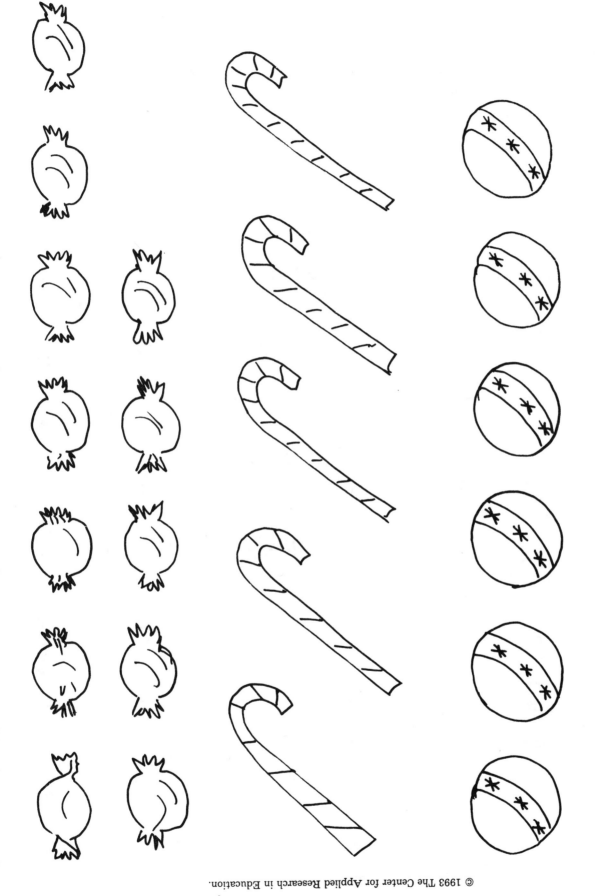

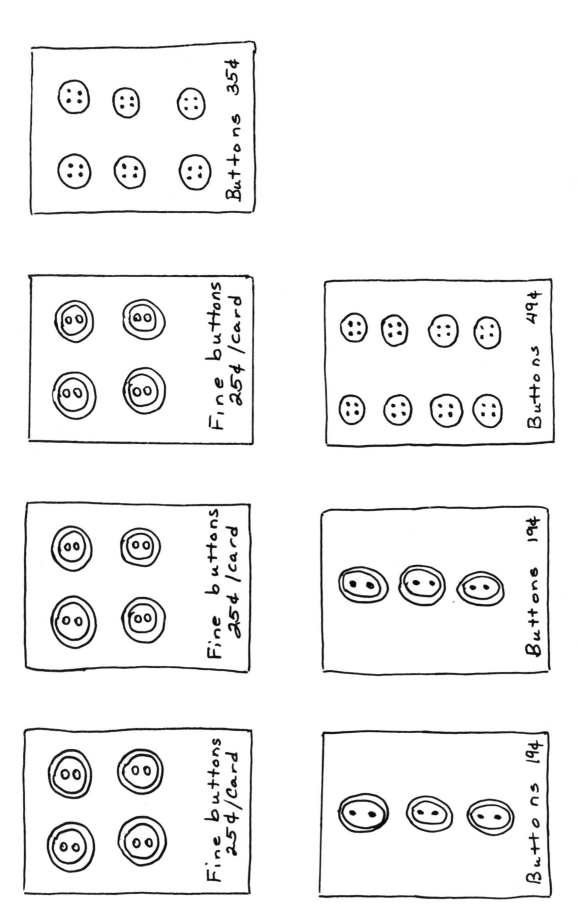

Buttons 35¢

Fine buttons 25¢/card

Buttons 49¢

Fine buttons 25¢/card

Buttons 19¢

Fine buttons 25¢/card

Buttons 19¢

2–8 STORY PROBLEMS—PICTURES FOR SET I

Name _____

You have a dozen _____
____. You use ____.
How many are left?
(Show how you got the answer on
the back.)

Grandma made ____
cupcakes. Then she
made ____ more. How
many does she have now? ____
(Show how you got the answer on
the back.)

**2–8 STORY PROBLEMS—SET II (CUT AND PASTE
ACTIVITY)**

There are ___ children.

You are going to form ___ teams.

How many children are on each team? ___

(Show solution on the back.)

There are ___ children.

Each child gets ___ cupcakes.

How many cupcakes will you need? ___

(Show solution on the back.)

You have ___ apples.

You get ___ more.

How many apples do you have now? ___

(Show solution on the back.)

There are ___ teams.

There are ___ children on each team.

How many children are playing?

___

(Show solution on the back.)

2–8 STORY PROBLEMS—SET II (CUT AND PASTE ACTIVITY)

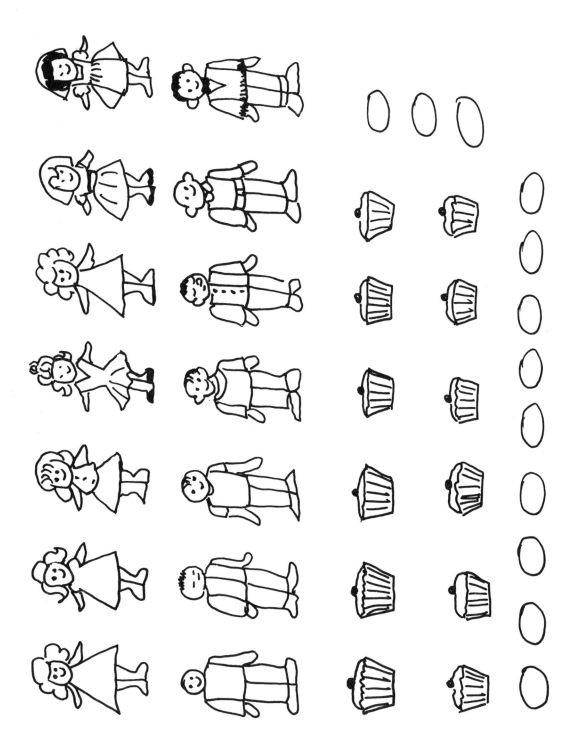

2–8 STORY PROBLEMS—PICTURES FOR SET II

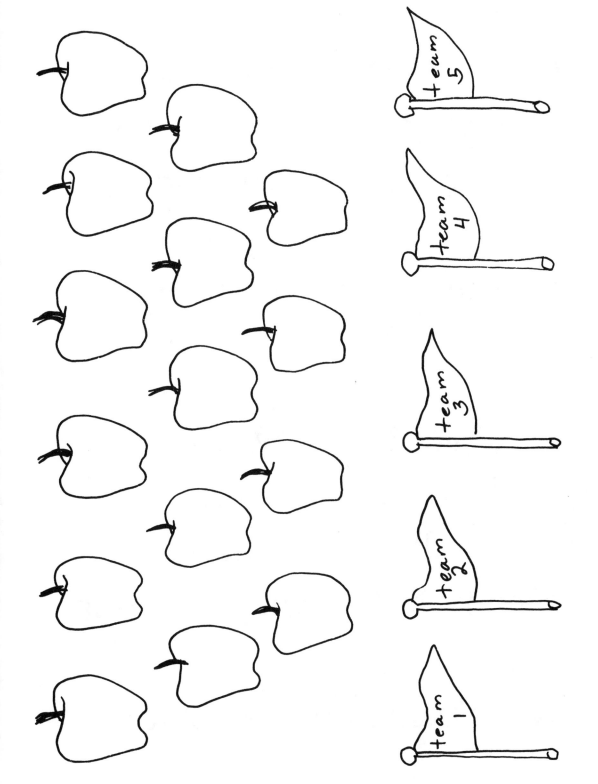

You must read ___ pages.

You have read ___.

How many are left to read?

___

(Show solution on the back.)

You are planting flowers.

If you have ___ pots and you

put ___ bulbs in each pot,

how many bulbs will you plant?

___

(Show solution on the back.)

2–8 STORY PROBLEMS—SET III (CUT AND PASTE ACTIVITY)

UNIT 3

Moving "Write" Along

Moving "Write" Along

Once children are reading at a functional level of 2.0, they are ready to broaden their horizons. While we continue reading to them and have them read to us, the primary thrust of this period is language arts development. We want to expand their opportunities to think, speak, and write.

3-1 INFERENTIAL THINKING

Objective: After reading a short selection, the child will be able to make reasonable predictions about what will happen next.

Rationale: Children have a great deal of trouble drawing inferences and making predictions. With practice, they usually show marked improvement in this ability.

Directions for Activity Sheets: In this section you will find two sets of cards. Set I is developed at about level 2.0 and is appropriate for use early in the school year. Set II is at reading level 2.7 and may be used at the end of the year. You may use the cards as homework or seatwork. Have the children do one to three cards. Each child writes an answer on the card. (If done as homework, a wider variety of answers tends to result.) Set aside classroom time so the children can formally share their reasoning and answers.

Name _____

Bill and his sister were not getting along. Bill called her a "big fat pig!"
> **What will happen next?**

Jane and her mother were walking by the pet store. There were kittens in one window and puppies in the other.
> **What will happen next?**

Tom and Jim were playing ball. The ball rolled into the street. Jim's mother came out of the house.
> **What will happen next?**

Mary was very tired. She had played hard all day. Daddy sat down to read to her. She began to rub eyes.
What will happen next?

Bob found a dime on the playground. He looked around. He could not tell who dropped it.
What will happen next?

Jon did not feel well. His head hurt. His throat was sore. First, he felt hot. Then, he felt cold.
What will happen next?

Daddy was painting. Little Sue was watching him. He went into the kitchen to eat lunch.
What will happen next?

It was mother's birthday. Ben did not have any money to buy a gift. He got some crayons and paper.
What will happen next?

Mrs. Green looked out in the backyard. She could not see her dog. She called but he did not come. Then she saw a hole under the fence.
What will happen next?

3–1 INFERENTIAL THINKING—SET I CARDS

Name _____

Father told Ben to clean his room. Ben kept on playing.

Mother told Ben to clean his room. Ben said, "I don't want to."

What will happen next?

A big orange cat was sleeping on the porch. The dog from next door ran up the porch steps. The cat woke up.

What will happen next?

The teacher stopped teaching. She frowned. She put her hands on her hips and stared at Sam.

What will happen next?

3–1 INFERENTIAL THINKING—SET I CARDS

Name _____

The sky was dark. It was filled with gray clouds. The wind blew. Lightning flashed. Thunder roared.
What will happen next?

Mike got his fishing rod. He looked for some sharp hooks. He bought some cheese. He dug up some worms. He and his mom drove to the lake.
What will happen next?

Ed was bored. He leaned back in his chair. Suddenly Ed felt like his world was turning upside down.
What will happen next?

Mr. Jones was trying to nail a new board to his fence, but it kept falling. He needed three hands—one to hold the nail, one to hold the board, and one to hammer.

Just then the postman came by.

What will happen next?

Ann rolled over to look at her clock. 7:30. "Oh, I'm late for school!" She jumped out of bed and started to dress. All at once it hit her. "Today is Saturday!"

What will happen next?

A huge deer stood in the meadow, eating the tall grass.

A hunter crept quietly toward the deer. The hunter raised his gun to aim.

A bird let out a loud squawk.

What will happen next?

3–1 INFERENTIAL THINKING—SET II CARDS

Name _____

> The books were put away. The desks had been cleaned out. The teacher was saying good-bye to the kids. Sally knew that tomorrow she could sleep late.
> **What will happen next?**

> Mother put some fried chicken, potato chips, and apples in a basket. She told us to get in the car. She began to drive out of town.
> **What will happen next?**

> Don was home alone. He fed the cat and went to bed. Just as he was falling asleep, he heard a noise. Someone was coming up the steps!
> **What will happen next?**

Brad wrote each word five times. He closed his eyes and said each letter. He turned his paper over and wrote each word again.

What will happen next?

Mother had been working in her garden. It was a hot day. She began to sweat.

When she came in, father said, "Your face is dirty and you don't smell good."

What will happen next?

Jack was hungry. He looked through the refrigerator. There were lots of leftovers. He opened a jar and began to drink out of it.

What will happen next?

3–2 WORD LIST
FOR FUNCTIONAL LEVEL 2

Begin a looseleaf notebook or folder for each child to keep in his or her desk. Put in copies of the Beginning Word List (Activity 2–3) from the previous unit and copies of the Word List for Functional Level 2. As the year proceeds, have the child add the other pages from this unit that will be marked "Notebook Materials." You will also want to send home a copy of these pages with a letter (you may use the same letter that is given in Activity 2–3).

Objective 1: The student will be able to recognize these words as well as the words in the Beginning Word List when they are presented randomly and without contextual clues.

Objective 2: The student will, by the end of the year, be able to spell the words from both lists accurately.

Rationale: The words chosen for these lists are those encountered most frequently in reading materials at grade levels 1 and 2. You will also note that these words constitute a large portion of the words used in casual adult writing, such as letters. Because of their extreme usefulness, we need to make every effort to help students learn to read and spell them.

When doing writing assignments, students may use these notebooks to assist them with spelling.

Word List

am	also	always
ate	after	around
any	again	about
bring	because	been
best	baby	both
buy	brought	better
clean	close	carry
draw	drink	different
ever	eight	early
even		
four	five	first
face	full	
garden	ground	

**3–2 WORD LIST FOR FUNCTIONAL LEVEL 2—
NOTEBOOK MATERIALS**

173

Word List (continued)

hand	head	hear
high	hold	hope
keep	kind	know
laugh	letter	left
many	money	men
morning	most	more
next	night	never
near	nine	
once	open	other
or	own	
people	place	pick
please		
quiet	quick	

**3–2 WORD LIST FOR FUNCTIONAL LEVEL 2—
NOTEBOOK MATERIALS (CONTINUED)**

Word List (continued)

six	seven	sister
start	send	such
should	story	street

thank	thought	then
think	they	three
try	their	together
these	those	today
ten		

under	until	upon

wash	wish	write
woman	while	watch

yesterday	year	

3–2 WORD LIST FOR FUNCTIONAL LEVEL 2— NOTEBOOK MATERIALS (CONTINUED)

3–3 STUDENT'S REMINDER FOR DECODING

Objective: The child will be able to decode one- and two-syllable words with the short and long vowel sounds as well as words that follow the vc/cv or the vc/ccv pattern or have special combinations.

Rationale: During this year the children will begin to encounter longer words in their reading. Since learning disabled students do not learn incidentally, you will need to plan some lessons that concentrate specifically on syllabication rules. For example, the child will need to be shown how to decode a word such as <u>became</u>. From previous learning he or she may understand that the first <u>e</u> says its name because of the bullying <u>a</u>, but you may need to explain the <u>e</u> on the end acts like a bully too to make the <u>a</u> say its name.

The student will also meet up with some vc/cv words such as <u>supper</u>. Ordinarily, the <u>e</u> would tell the <u>u</u> to say its name. Right? Wrong. When a word has the vc/cv configuration, it breaks into two syllables—<u>sup</u> + <u>per</u>. Tell the children that the <u>e</u> wants to make the <u>u</u> say its name but it can't because there is a wall between the consonants and the <u>u</u> can't get over it. So it is with vc/ccv, as in <u>mid</u> + <u>dle</u>.

The two sounds for <u>c</u> and g will also need to be carefully taught.

Directions: This is a notebook page to add to the folder.

Student's Reminder for Decoding

Rule 1: Count the vowels.

If there is one: a = 🍎   e 🎋 ^edge   i = itch

o = 🐙   u = ↑

Rule 2: Watch for vc/cv and vc/ccv.

If there is, the word breaks into syllables. Example: bet/ter

vccv

Otherwise, bē cāme

Rule 3: Watch for combinations.

sh = ⭐

ch = 🪑 or k

th = 👄

ph = f

er   as in

ir   her

ur   girl

burn

or = as in for

ar = as in 🚗 car

wr = wr

kn = kn

gh = ghost

night

laugh(f)

oo = as in too

ing = thing

ou = out

al = all

oi/oy = as in

boy or oil

c = k

ce

ci } says

cy } s

ow { as in now

{ or snōw

au/aw = saw

g = go

tion/sion = shun

y = yes

my(ī)

happy(ē)

ge } may

gi } say

gy } j

3–3 STUDENT'S REMINDER FOR DECODING— NOTEBOOK MATERIALS

3–4 VOWEL SOUNDS AND PATTERNS

Activity 2–1C in Unit Two gives you materials for a bulletin board display of vowel sounds and an illustration of how that bulletin board might look.

In this section you will find activity sheets that remind students that words have patterns and many words belong to a word family. This means that if you can spell one word in the family, you will be able to spell the others (for example, look, book, took, cook, shook, hook).

Objective: The student will demonstrate a knowledge of vowel patterns by classifying words according to their vowel pattern.

Rationale: Once learned, a knowledge of vowel patterns can help with spelling. For example, the child wants to spell a word, such as coat, but he cannot remember the letters. He hears "c.o.t." He knows that for the o to say its name, there must be another vowel. You encourage the child to look at the bulletin board. On paper, he writes cote, coat, cowt (the three common patterns). At this point he may say, "Oh, I see. It's coat." Remind him of boat; show him float.

Directions for Activity Sheets: The first page is for the child's folder. For the next worksheet, have the child classify each word by its pattern.

Vowel Sounds and Patterns

Name _____

Common Vowel Patterns

a_e	**ai**	**ay**
_____	_____	_____
_____	_____	_____
_____	_____	_____

o_e	**oa**	**ow**
_____	_____	_____
_____	_____	_____

ue	**ui**	_____
_____	_____	
_____	_____	

rain	day	play
show	take	rope
coat	paint	suit
blue	fruit	say
make	true	boat
snow	row	hope
	wake	

3–4 VOWEL SOUNDS AND PATTERNS

3–5 ANTONYMS

Objective: When given a word from the lists found in this book, the student will give its antonym.

Rationale: These activities are designed to help the child understand what an antonym is and to expand his or her knowledge in that area. It represents another language development activity.

Directions for Activity Sheets: You will find a notebook page to be added to the student's desk folder. It defines the word and gives some examples. The section also includes some practice sheets.

Extension: Students enjoy making a game of these sheets. After several experiences with a given list of words, you can have races. Pair students of similar abilities and have one winner per pair. Insist on correct spelling of the antonym so the child can receive credit for it. The same list can be done again and again, with the child competing only with himself or herself by keeping a graph and watching any improvements. A small reward can enhance effort.

In their notebook, the students keep a running list of all antonyms they meet during the year. An antonym bulletin board can be fun if you let students add new words as they find them. Each addition allows you to do a minilesson to remind them what an antonym is.

Antonyms

Antonyms are words that <u>do</u> <u>not</u> mean the same thing. They are opposites.

come	give	up
go	take	down

come ⟶

go ⟵

Name _____

Antonyms

in ____   lost _____

big _____   wet ____

open _____   tall _____

now _____   stop __

off __   dark _____

hot _____   girl ___

day _____   mine _____

give _____   first _____

up _____   front _____

work _____   fast _____

on	close	found
go	cold	yours
out	take	night
boy	down	light
dry	last	short
little	slow	later
	play	back

Antonyms

good ____   many ____
rise _____   noisy _____
here _____   shout _____
left _____   come ___
over _____   man _____
wild _____   push _____
short _____   dirty _____
black _____   soft _____
happy ____   rich _____
high ____   adult _____

go	fall	there	quiet
bad	long	right	under
hard	pull	child	clean
sad	poor	woman	white
few	low	tame	whisper

3–5 ANTONYMS

Name _____

3–5 ANTONYMS

over
here _____

rich
high _____

noisy
short _____

adult
wild _____

rise
soft _____

good
come _____

man
push _____

dirty
left _____

shout
many _____

happy
work _____

3–5 ANTONYMS

3–6 HOMOPHONES

Some time this year you will want to deal with homophones. "Homo" means *same* and "phone" means *sound;* therefore, homophones are words that sound alike. They are not spelled alike, and they do not mean the same thing.

Objective: The student will be able to read the homophones contained here and explain what each word means.

Rationale: Again, we are helping the student develop knowledge about our language.

Directions for Activity Sheets: You will find a notebook page for the child's folder and two activity sheets for the child to complete.

Extension: As with antonyms, you will want to encourage students to add new words to their homophone lists throughout the year.

Homophones

Homophones are words that sound the same, but they don't mean the same thing. They are also spelled differently.

Examples:

c = a letter of the alphabet
see = to see with your 👁
sea = water 〰〰〰

Name _____

① On Sunday we will take our boat and go for
   a _____. (sale/sail)

② I want you to sit over _____ (there, their) by her.

③ Dad went to the store and I went _____. (to, two, too)

④ The _____ (plane, plain) was high in the sky.

⑤ She read to me. The story was a _____ (tail, tale) about a rabbit named Peter.

3–6 HOMOPHONES

Name _____

① I was happy to _____ (see, sea) him.
② She gave me a _____ (piece, peace) of cake.
③ There were five letters in the _____ (male, mail) today.
④ Some people don't eat _____ (meat, meet)
⑤ Can you _____ (hear, here) what she is saying?

3–6 HOMOPHONES

3–7 SYNONYMS

Objective: The student will give a correct synonym for 25 words.

Rationale: The teaching of synonyms begins early and continues throughout the child's school career. We tell children to read something and paraphrase what they read. For a person to "put it in his or her own words" requires synonyms.

Directions: Insert the notebook page into the student's folder.

Extension: Looking up words in the dictionary and writing their synonyms is an incredibly boring task. Worse yet, it is a waste of time because most children do not learn much from it.

A far more productive approach is having them play the Synonym Game. Construct a game board (see the following illustration) from a large piece of heavy paper and laminate it if possible.

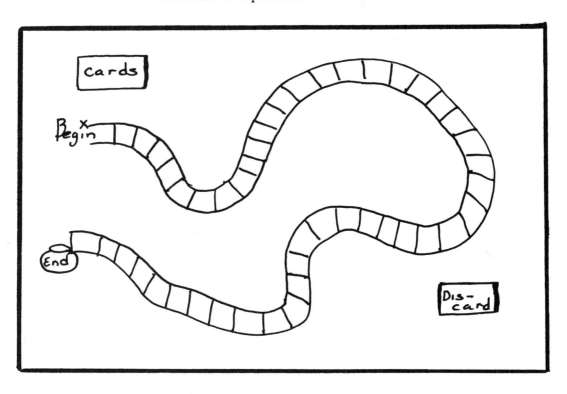

Using 2″ × 3″ cards, put one synonym on each card, and make a master list of all the synonyms you are using. (A sample synonyms list is given.) Spend several days talking about the words. The children need to be able to read the words; otherwise, they will not be able to play the game without adult help.

Three children (two opponents and one referee) can play at each board. The referee reads the word list to both players before the play begins. After the play begins, the word list should be kept on a clipboard that only the referee can see. His or her job is to check the accuracy of the players' answers.

After deciding who will play first, the first player draws a card. Player One is allowed to move one space for each correct synonym he or she can give for the word on the card. If Player One can give all the synonyms for a given word, he or she may take another card. This continues as long as Player One can give *all* the synonyms for a word. If Player One cannot give all the synonyms, he or she discards, and it is Player Two's turn. Play continues until someone reaches the *End*. The winner switches places with the referee, and a new game begins. I use lemon drops to ensure diligent play; each player gets one and the winner gets two.

The cards can be used a second way. Using a red pen, make an additional set of cards that have the synonyms. Have the student lay out the red synonym cards and then match them with the word cards.

Synonyms

afraid—scared, frightened
amaze—surprise, astonish
angry—mad
bellow—roar, yell, shout, scream
big—large, huge, giant, enormous
boulder—rock, stone
delicious—good, tasty
doze—sleeping, napping
exhausted—tired, weary
fast—swift, rapid, quickly
finish—complete, end
horrible—awful, terrible, bad
job—task, chore, work
kind—helpful, gentle, generous
little—tiny, small
lodges—caught, stuck
odor—smell, scent
path—trail, walkway
pretty—beautiful, lovely
shine—glisten, glow, sparkle
squirm—twist, wiggle
stumble—trip, falter
suggest—advise, tell
tremble—shake, quiver
whole—entire, all

3–7 SYNONYMS—SAMPLE WORD LIST

Synonyms

Synonyms are words that mean the same thing.

Examples:

big
large
huge

small
tiny
little

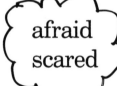

afraid
scared

shut
close

I was <u>afraid</u>.
means the same as
I was <u>scared</u>.

3–8 SIX IMPORTANT QUESTIONS

Objective: The child will understand what the words <u>who</u>, <u>what</u>, <u>where</u>, <u>why</u>, <u>when</u>, and <u>how</u> mean. He or she will demonstrate that understanding by correctly answering the questions on the last activity sheet in this section.

Rationale: When I first started teaching, I thought children knew what these words meant. Some do, some don't.

First, you want them to know that when a sentence begins with one of these words, the sentence is always a question and will have a question mark at the end. You also want them to know that these are probably the most important questions because good writing always gives the information to answer them.

Directions: You will need to do some preliminary work before having the children use the activity sheets in this section. The children need to understand that <u>who</u> means a person, <u>where</u> refers to a place, <u>why</u> refers to a reason for an action, and <u>when</u> is a time. A birthday party invitation is a good example to use.

? ? ? ? ? ?

? **Words That** ?

Signal

? **Questions** ?

<u>W</u>hat   <u>W</u>ho   <u>W</u>here
<u>W</u>hen   <u>W</u>hy   <u>W</u>hich

Are   Have
Can   Has
Do   How
Does   Is
Did   Will

**3–8 SIX IMPORTANT QUESTIONS—
NOTEBOOK MATERIALS**

Name _____

Directions: Read the story. Using the information given, answer each question.

Tom felt bad all day. His stomach hurt. As soon as school was out, he hurried home and went to bed. Tom's mother kept coming into his room to look in on him because she was worried about him.

<u>Who</u> was sick?

<u>What</u> was wrong with him?

<u>When</u> did he go to bed?

<u>Where</u> was he when he got sick?

<u>How</u> long was he sick before he went to bed?

<u>Why</u> did his mother keep looking at him?

Name _____

Directions: Read the story. Using the information given, answer each question.

Bill loved flowers. He asked his mom if he could make a garden in the backyard. She told him he could plant one in the far corner of the yard. First, he got some seeds that he could plant in December. He loosened the dirt and very carefully placed them six inches apart. Very quickly, the seeds grew into plants with tiny white flowers.

Who planted the garden?

What did he plant?

Why did he plant the seeds?

When did he plant them?

How did he plant them?

Where did he plant them?

© 1993 The Center for Applied Research in Education.

3–8 SIX IMPORTANT QUESTIONS—STORY TWO

Name _____

Directions: Read the story. Using the information given, answer each question.

Mr. Green was looking for a job. He wanted to be a firefighter because he liked to help people. He took some tests at the firehouse to show he was strong. On Monday he found out that he had passed. He was very happy.

<u>Who</u> wanted the job?

<u>What</u> job did he want?

<u>Why</u> did he choose that job?

<u>Where</u> did he go to take a test?

<u>When</u> did he learn that he got the job?

<u>How</u> did he feel when he got the job?

3–8 SIX IMPORTANT QUESTIONS—STORY THREE

Name _____

Directions: Read the story. Using the information given, answer
each question.

　　　　Mrs. Jones was having some friends over for
dinner. She knew they would like the pecan pie she
always made. First, she made a crust. Next, she
made the filling. Finally, she carefully laid a layer of
pecans on top.
　　　　She baked the pie and then put it on the window
ledge to cool while she dressed in her best clothes.
　　　　At six o'clock her friends rang the doorbell.

<u>Who</u> baked the pie?

<u>What</u> kind of pie was it?

<u>Why</u> did she make it?

<u>When</u> did she make it?

<u>Where</u> did she put the pie to cool?

<u>How</u> did she put the pecans on the pie?

Name _____

Directions: Read the story. Using the information given, answer each question.

Mother wanted to get Jane something really nice for her birthday. She knew that Jane liked dresses that had animals on them. She found a cute red dress with a white duck on it at the store. On the day before her birthday, Mother gave the dress to Jane. "Jane, I'm giving this to you early so you can wear it for your party." Jane was very pleased with the new dress.

Who got a new dress?

What color was it?

Where did the dress come from?

Why did Jane's mother choose that dress?

When did Jane's mother give it to Jane?

How did Jane feel about the dress?

3-9 PUNCTUATION

Objective: The student will punctuate a set of statements and questions accurately.

Rationale: Teachers find it frustrating because learning disabled children have difficulty deciding whether to use a period or a question mark at the end of a sentence.

Directions: The children will need the notebook page, "Words That Signal Questions," from Activity 3-8. Teach the children to look for and recognize key words at the start of sentences that signal the sentence is a question. You will find three practice activity sheets to get you started. They are easy to construct, and if you need more, you can make up your own (even putting in the words from your current reading or spelling list).

Name _____

Directions:

1. <u>Underline</u> the first word of each sentence.
2. Look at the chart of words that signal questions.
3. Is the underlined word there?
   If <u>yes</u>, put a question mark (?) at the end of the sentence.
   If <u>no</u>, put a period (.) at the end of the sentence.

Is your room clean _____

The store is full of people _____

Did you take a bath _____

What is your name _____

You will need a coat _____

Why is the baby crying _____

Where is mom now _____

Can I plant these seeds _____

How did you make that _____

After dinner, I will play _____

Does she work _____

Which one do you want _____

3–9 PUNCTUATION

Name _____

Directions:

1. <u>Underline</u> the first word of each sentence.
2. <u>Look</u> at the chart of words that signal questions.
3. Is the underlined word there?

   If <u>yes</u>, put a question mark (?) at the end of the sentence.

   If <u>no</u>, put a period (.) at the end of the sentence.

My new coat is blue _____

Do you want to play a game _____

Are you sick _____

Is she here _____

Can I see your paper _____

How old are you _____

My friend is very nice _____

Who said that _____

When is he coming _____

Has he had his dinner _____

Will you help me _____

I like to play ball _____

3–9 PUNCTUATION

Name _____

Directions:

1. <u>Underline</u> the first word of each sentence.
2. <u>Look</u> at the chart of words that signal questions.
3. Is the underlined word there?
   If <u>yes</u>, put a question mark (?) at the end of the sentence.
   If <u>no</u>, put a period (.) at the end of the sentence.

What day is it _____
Are you going with me _____
He is my friend _____
Where is my book _____

It is time to get up _____
Did you see him fall down _____
Is this your pen _____
Why did you leave _____

How do you like the cake _____
We went to see him _____
Does he look like you _____
Which way did he go _____

3–9 PUNCTUATION

3–10 CAPITALIZATION

Objective: The child will show an awareness of three capitalization rules:

Rule 1—Capitalize the first word of a sentence.

Rule 2—Capitalize all proper names.

Rule 3—Capitalize the personal pronoun I.

Rationale: You probably introduced these rules in grade 1, but this year we want to try to get them to be habits. As with establishing any habit, you will need to practice it regularly.

Directions: Since most children must do something 90 times to know it, you may want to spend 10 minutes every day looking at sentences similar to the ones on the worksheets and having students come to the board and explain why we had to capitalize each underlined word. (The numbers under the sentences refer to the three rules.) The worksheets could be used either as a pretest or a posttest.

Guided Practice

1. Mary and I went to New York.
   <u>1,2</u>   <u>3</u>   <u>2</u> <u>2</u>

2. We saw the movie Snow White.
   <u>1</u>   <u>2</u> <u>2</u>

3. On Sunday, there is no school.
   <u>1</u> <u>2</u>

Independent Practice—Lesson 1

1. My birthday falls on Monday.

   —   —

2. Aunt Sue is coming for a visit.

   —   —

3. Our school team is called the Giants.

   —   —

Independent Practice—Lesson 2

1. The book <u>Our World</u> is lost.

   — — —

2. Can I play with Bill?

   — —   —

3. Next month is April.

   —   —

3–10 CAPITALIZATION

3–11 FIVE ELEMENTS OF A GOOD SENTENCE

In previous lessons you have covered capitalization and punctuation. Now we will introduce students to the concepts *noun, verb,* and *phrase.* You may have used these previously, but now we teach a little more about them.

Objective 1: The child will be able to name the five elements of a good sentence.

Objective 2: When shown a sentence containing only a subject-noun, verb, and a phrase, the child will be able to identify the three parts. (The child may use his or her notebook pages to help.)

Rationale: Our purpose this year is to introduce these concepts. We will not expect mastery until sometime into the fifth grade. Out of these activities we hope students will begin to build more interesting sentences.

Directions: To introduce the concept of nouns, you can play "It's a bird! It's a plane! It's Superman!" The fun in this game is its rapid-fire nature. You go down the row and have each child name some object that he or she can draw. Tell the children that all the words are *nouns.* On the next day, pair children. They are to list as many nouns as they can in 5 minutes. Finally, on the activity sheet you find here, help the children list names of people (proper names of their friends) and other commonly used nouns. This activity sheet will then become a referent for the future. Similarly, help the children list *places* such as home, school, church, park, store, and post office as well as places they go to (personalize list). Under *things,* help them list some common items such as tree, car, cat and so on.

In this section you will find three more pages to be put into the student's desk folder. The pages may be enlarged to use as a classroom bulletin board.

One of the notebook pages lists helping verbs as well as some action verbs. For familiarizing children with these, you can have children scan printed material and circle all the helping verbs they can find. They are allowed to work alone or with a friend. Make it a contest.

To illustrate how phrases act, put the following words on the board:

I am . . . (show them what phrases can do).

I am <u>over here</u>.

I am <u>seven years old</u>.

I am <u>on the phone</u>.

Five Elements of a Good Sentence

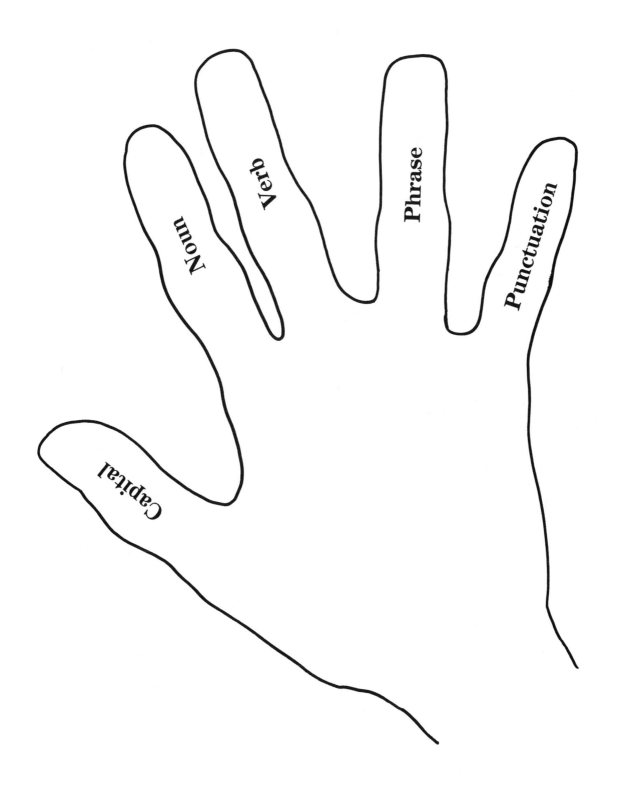

3–11 FIVE ELEMENTS OF A GOOD SENTENCE— NOTEBOOK MATERIALS

Name _____

Nouns are the names of people, places, or things.

people

places

things

people	places	things
1. Mother	1. _____	1. _____
2. Daddy	2. _____	2. _____
3. sister	3. _____	3. _____
4. brother	4. _____	4. _____
5. baby	5. _____	5. _____
6. _____	6. _____	6. _____
7. _____	7. _____	7. _____
8. _____	8. _____	8. _____
9. _____	9. _____	9. _____
10. _____	10. _____	10. _____

3–11 FIVE ELEMENTS OF A GOOD SENTENCE— NOTEBOOK MATERIALS

Name _____

Predicates (also called verbs)

Helping Verbs	Some Doing Verbs
am	eat
are	sleep
be	help
been	wash
being	walk
can/can't	talk
could/couldn't	play
do/don't	work
did/didn't	go
does/doesn't	run
had/hadn't	sit
has/hasn't	fall
have/haven't	write
is/isn't	fold
may	jump
must	cut
might	draw
should/shouldn't	print
was/wasn't	underline
were/weren't	read
will/won't	circle
would/wouldn't	and many more

3–11 FIVE ELEMENTS OF A GOOD SENTENCE— NOTEBOOK MATERIALS

Name _____

Directions: These sentence fragments need a phrase added so that they make sense. Your teacher will help you.

1. I am _____.

2. She can see _____.

3. Bill doesn't like to _____.

4. My sister won't help me _____.

5. We were quiet because _____
_____.

6. Mother told me I must clean _____.

7. Will you go to _____?

3–11 FIVE ELEMENTS OF A GOOD SENTENCE—PHRASES

Name _____

Directions: Use each phrase to make a sentence.

on my bed		at six o'clock
to the movie		with my friend
	because it was cold	

1. _____
   _____

2. _____
   _____

3. _____
   _____

4. _____
   _____

5. _____
   _____

3–11 FIVE ELEMENTS OF A GOOD SENTENCE—PHRASES

3-12 ALPHABETIZING

Objective: The student will alphabetize ten word lists using the second letter where necessary.

Rationale: This skill is a prerequisite to dictionary use or filing.

Directions for Activity Sheets: Have students circle the first letter of each word and arrange these into proper order. Then have them look at the words that begin with the same letter to see what the second letter is.

Name _____

Directions: • Circle the first letter of each word.
• Alphabetize by the first letter.
• Look at the second letters of the two words that have the same beginning letter.
• List the words in order, using the second letters to help.

1. baby   b _____

2. garden   b _____

3. left   g _____

4. keep   g _____

5. best   k _____

6. ground   k _____

7. live   l _____

8. people   l _____

9. know   p _____

10. place   p _____

3–12 ALPHABETIZING

Name _____

Directions:
- Circle the first letter of each word.
- Alphabetize by the first letter.
- Look at the second letters of the two words that have the same beginning letter.
- List the words in order, using the second letters to help.

1. once

2. head

3. try

4. hand

5. letter

6. clean

7. carry

8. open

9. kind

10. together

_____

_____

_____

_____

_____

_____

_____

_____

_____

_____

3–12 ALPHABETIZING

Name _____

Directions: • Circle the first letter of each word.
• Alphabetize by the first letter.
• Look at the second letters of the two words that have the same beginning letter.
• List the words in order, using the second letters to help.

1. yesterday   _____

2. bring   _____

3. under   _____

4. five   _____

5. upon   _____

6. many   _____

7. ever   _____

8. face   _____

9. such   _____

10. most   _____

3–13 COMPREHENSION

Objective 1: The student will demonstrate he or she is reading at the functional level of 2.0 as measured by a standardized test.

Rationale: These activity sheets are designed so that children will be aware that each word in a sentence affects its meaning. They can be used as a warm-up exercise immediately prior to giving a standardized reading test, such as the Woodcock, Piat. You can also use them for less formal diagnostic purposes. All words on the worksheets were covered in Unit One or are totally decodable by the one- or two-vowel rules. If a student can read every word correctly and locate the correct picture, he or she is functioning in the 2.0 range.

Objective 2: The student will demonstrate he or she is reading at a functional level of 2.5 by reading these worksheets aloud and finding the picture that matches the words.

Rationale: If the child can decode all these words and find the right picture, you are assured that he or she is making steady progress.

Extension: To become good readers, it is a cardinal rule that children must read every day. My students are required to read aloud 15 minutes a day. I listen to some, my tutor listens to others, and I have a group of cross-aged tutors (fourth and fifth graders—some are older learning disabled students) who listen to those who are reading without struggling. The Barnell-Loft *Multiple Skills* series mentioned earlier comes with comprehension questions, which are helpful in checking daily comprehension.

Name _____

Directions: Read the sentence. Find the picture that shows what the words mean.

1. Two men are painting a house.

2. The boy on the bike took our picture.

3. The boys and girls sat near the water.

3–13 COMPREHENSION (2.0)

Directions: Read the sentence. Find the picture that shows what the words mean.

4. The men were playing ball.

5. Mother was working at her desk.

6. After a long ride, they were tired.

3–13 COMPREHENSION (2.0)

Directions: Read the sentence. Find the picture that shows what the words mean.

7. The diver jumped from the boat.

8. Mother takes good care of her plants.

3–13 COMPREHENSION (2.0)

Name _____

Directions: Match the sentences with the pictures.

The plane was coming in for a landing.	The man used ski poles to go down the mountain.
It was so hard for him to get up that Mr. Brown vowed to get to bed earlier.	The couple went walking every evening.

3–13 COMPREHENSION (2.5)

Name _____

Directions: Match the sentences with the pictures.

When she went for a ride on her bike, her dog often followed her.	The couple enjoyed eating out in restaurants.
In this game, the ball is moved with the feet.	Climbing poles is part of this man's job.

Directions: Match the sentences with the pictures.

The heavy clouds brought rain and lightning.	The music was so loud, it hurt my ears.
At the sound of the shot, the boy started to run.	He ran across the floor with the ball.

3–13 COMPREHENSION (2.5)

Name _____

Directions: Match the sentences with the pictures.

A swarm of bees tried to sting them.	A flat tire caused the car to crash.
The powerful motor sent the boat flying through the water.	Mr. Jones likes to cook for his family.

3–13 COMPREHENSION (2.5)—
PICTURES TO CUT OUT

3–13 COMPREHENSION (2.5)—
PICTURES TO CUT OUT

3-14 WRITING PARAGRAPHS

Objective: When given a main idea, the student will write at least two supporting details.

Rationale: This section represents an introduction to paragraph writing. It is not intended to render the child proficient at this task, but only to open an awareness to the idea of paragraphing and to give an exposure to some of the terms. The child will continue to work on this skill every year.

Directions: In Set I of the worksheets, there are pictures and sentences that the student arranges into a paragraph. There is a built-in title, margin, and indenting. The child does not even have to make up his or her own sentences. After cutting the sentences out, the child arranges them in a logical order. It is hoped that, as you check them, you will also have time to have the child read them to you before he or she copies them.

In Set II of the worksheets, the sentences are again given to be cut and arranged. At this point, however, you need to talk about *indenting*. After writing the sentences, you will discuss how to get a *title*. Here is where you explain that titles are short and each word needs to be capitalized.

In Set III, the student is asked to generate his or her own supporting details. Pictures are given for those students who need input, but be careful not to stifle creativity. If a child is able to create his or her own details, let the child do so.

As the student moves through this section, the number of clues is gradually reduced and the child is called upon to do more critical thinking. By the time the child reaches the worksheet entitled "Lost Dog/Found Dog" (set IV), the child can be introduced to the paragraph cluster. First, the child writes a main idea in the center. Next, he or she brainstorms for supporting details about the main idea. Using a spoke, the child writes two or three words to remind himself or herself of the idea. After brainstorming, he or she goes back and decides which details he or she wants to use, crossing off the ones he or she doesn't want. Then the child numbers the usable ideas in the order he or she wants. Now the child writes the paragraph. Each prong represents one sentence, so as he or she writes, the child will punctuate at the end of that idea (before going on to the next prong).

Here is an example of how a cluster works.

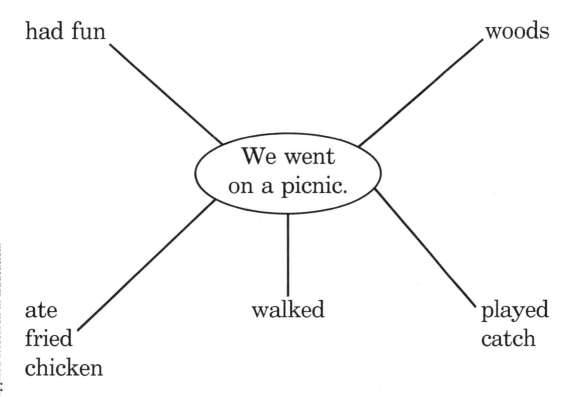

When written in paragraph form, it converts to this:

A Picnic

We went on a picnic today. We drove to the woods. We ate fried chicken. We played catch. Then we took a walk on some trails in the woods. We had fun.

Writing Paragraphs

Preplan
- Choose a topic.
- List your ideas.
- Decide on a main idea.
- Plan the order of your paragraph.

Writing
- Margins
- Indenting
- Main idea followed by details

Editing
- Reread for sense.
- Reread for spelling.
- Reread for capitalization/punctuation.
- Rewrite for neatness.

3-14 WRITING PARAGRAPHS—NOTEBOOK MATERIALS

Name _____

Directions:

- Cut out the sentences below.
- Arrange them so that they make sense.
- Have your teacher check your plan.
- Copy the sentences.

The Kite

_____
_____
_____
_____
_____
_____

| Mary made a kite. |
| It got stuck in a tree. |
| The wind took the kite up. |

3–14 WRITING PARAGRAPHS—SET I

Name _____

Directions:
- Cut out the sentences below.
- Arrange them so that they make sense.
- Have your teacher check your plan.
- Copy the sentences.

My Friend

_____

_____

_____

_____

_____

_____

First we played hopscotch.
Then we had a snack.
My friend came over to play.

Name _____

Directions:

- Cut out the sentences below.
- Arrange them so that they make sense.
- Have your teacher check your plan.
- Copy the sentences.

The Baby Birds

_____

_____

_____

_____

_____

_____

| She made a nest in our tree. |
| One morning I saw a bird. |
| She laid two eggs. |
| In a few days, the eggs hatched. |

3–14 WRITING PARAGRAPHS—SET I   233

Name _____

Directions:

- Cut out the sentences below.
- Arrange them so that they make sense.
- Have your teacher check your plan.
- Copy your sentences.

A New Book

_____

_____

_____

_____

_____

_____

He loved the pictures.
She gave it to her son.
Mother bought a book on sharks.
He read it over and over.

3–14 WRITING PARAGRAPHS—SET I   234

Name _____

_____

_____

_____

_____

_____

_____

_____

_____

_____

_____

Directions to the Teacher:

- Cut the sentences along the lines.
- Place them in an envelope labeled "Saturdays."
- Have the student arrange the sentences and write a paragraph on the page provided.

Saturdays are busy at our house.
Dad cuts the grass.
Jason does the wash.
I clean my room.

For more able students, add:

We have lunch out.
In the afternoon, we go to the park or to a show.

3–14 WRITING PARAGRAPHS—SET II

Directions to the Teacher:

- Cut the sentences along the lines.
- Place them in an envelope labeled "Jan's Garden."
- Have the student arrange the sentences and write a paragraph on the page provided.

Jan wanted a garden.

Mother got her some seeds.

Jan planted them.

In about a week, she saw little green sprouts coming up.

For more able students, add:

She watered them every day.

She loved picking the flowers she had grown.

3–14 WRITING PARAGRAPHS—SET II

Directions to the Teacher:
- Cut the sentences along the lines.
- Place them in an envelope labeled "Making Bread."
- Have the student arrange the sentences and write a paragraph on the page provided.

© 1993 The Center for Applied Research in Education.

Mother wants to make bread.
First, she got out all the things she would need and turned the oven on.
She mixed the batter, poured it in pans, and put the pans in the oven to bake.
The homemade bread was so good with jam and butter.

For more able students, add:

I watched how she did it.
She says I can make some next week.

Directions to the Teacher:

- Cut the sentences along the lines.
- Place them in an envelope labeled "Scared."
- Have the student arrange the sentences and write a paragraph on the page provided.

What was that noise?
I sat up in my bed and listened as hard as I could.
I was so scared I couldn't even scream.
Suddenly my cat jumped on the bed.

For more able students, add:

It was the middle of the night.
I was home all alone.

Directions to the Teacher:

- Cut the sentences along the lines.
- Place them in an envelope labeled "Hide and Seek."
- Have the student arrange the sentences and write a paragraph on the page provided.

We decided to play hide and seek.
I said I would be "It."
I closed my eyes and counted to one hundred.
I found everyone very quickly.

For more able students, add:

"Coming, ready or not!" I yelled.
We need to think of some new hiding places.

Name _____

Directions: Write at least four supporting details for this main idea.

Alone

There are many things you can do when you are all by yourself. _____

_____

_____

_____

_____

_____

_____

_____

_____

3–14 WRITING PARAGRAPHS—SET III 241

Name _____

Directions: Write at least three supporting details for this main idea.

Vacation

When vacation comes, I have no trouble keeping busy.

_____

_____

_____

_____

_____

_____

_____

_____

_____

3–14 WRITING PARAGRAPHS—SET III

Name _____

Directions: Write at least three supporting details for this main
idea.

Animal Homes

Animal homes can be found almost anywhere. _____

_____

_____

_____

_____

_____

_____

_____

_____

3–14 WRITING PARAGRAPHS—SET III

Name _____

Directions: Write at least three supporting ideas for this main
idea.

A Walk in the Woods

My friend and I went for a walk in the woods. _____

_____

_____

_____

_____

_____

_____

_____

Name _____

Directions: Write at least three supporting ideas for this main idea.

Angry

When I am mad, I find ways to get rid of my anger. —

_____

_____

_____

_____

_____

_____

_____

_____

3-14 WRITING PARAGRAPHS—SET III

Name _____

Directions: Use an idea cluster. Then write at least three details
to go with the main idea.

Lost Dog/Found Dog

One day I could not find my dog. _____

_____

_____

_____

_____

_____

_____

_____

© 1993 The Center for Applied Research in Education.

3-14 WRITING PARAGRAPHS—SET IV

Name _____

Directions: Use an idea cluster. Then write at least three
supporting details for the main idea. Who will race?
What kind of race? How did it come out?

Racing

"Let's have a race!" _____

_____

_____

_____

_____

_____

_____

_____

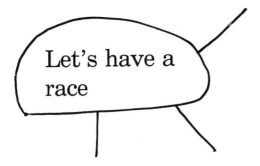

Name _____

Directions: Use an idea cluster. Then write three supporting details for the main idea. What kind of pet? What is special about it?

Our New Pet

We have a new pet. _____

_____

_____

_____

_____

_____

_____

_____

3-15 NUMBER WORDS

Objective: The student will demonstrate an understanding of the meaning of number words by converting number words into numbers and by converting numbers into number words.

Rationale: This section is being included because this is primarily a reading skill, involving converting words to numbers, and vice versa.

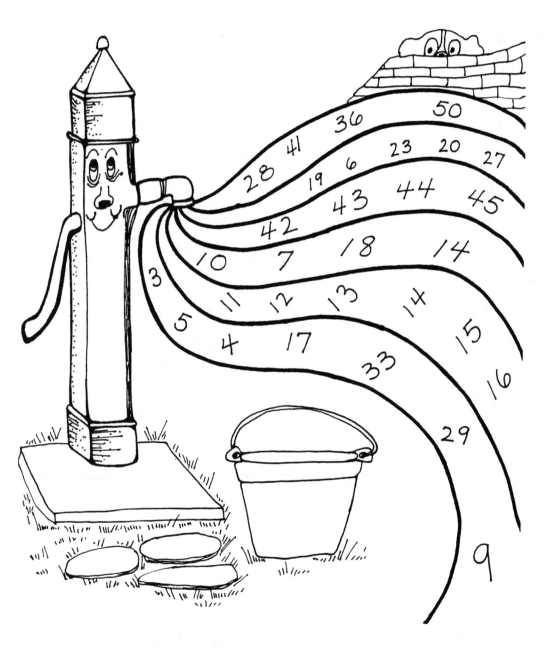

Number Words

1—one	16—sixteen
2—two	17—seventeen
3—three	18—eighteen
4—four	19—nineteen
5—five	20—twenty
6—six	30—thirty
7—seven	40—forty
8—eight	50—fifty
9—nine	60—sixty
10—ten	70—seventy
11—eleven	80—eighty
12—twelve	90—ninety
13—thirteen	100—hundred
14—fourteen	1,000—thousand
15—fifteen	

3–15 NUMBER WORDS—NOTEBOOK MATERIALS

Name _____

Sample: Write 215 in words.
Use your notebook page to help.

Two hundred fifteen _____

1. Write 652 in words.

_____

STOP Let your teacher check your answer.

2. Write 72 in words.

_____

STOP Let your teacher check your answer.

3. Write 105 in words.

_____

STOP Let your teacher check your answer.

4. Write _____ in words.

_____

5. Write _____ in words.

_____

3–15 NUMBER WORDS

Name _____

Sample: Turn number words into digits.
Use your notebook page to help.

Nine hundred thirteen ___

Seventy-six ___

Three hundred four ___

Eight hundred forty-two ___

Seventeen ___

_____ ___

_____ ___

_____ ___

_____ ___

3–15 NUMBER WORDS

3–16 NUMBER PROBLEMS

Objective: The student will be able to solve number problems and show how the problem was done.

Rationale: Solving number problems is being able to understand what the words mean, which is a reading skill.

Directions: In Unit Two, students were asked in Activity 2-8 to cut and paste to illustrate how they solved their problems. If your students did not participate in those activities, you may want to use them before using the following worksheets. This section asks the students to convert the words into mental images and draw their own pictures. Blanks are left so that the worksheets can be used again and again throughout the year. All you need to do is change the numbers.

In answering the problem, it is recommended that the students write their answers in words instead of numbers. This will help students learn to spell number words.

Extension: To help the child to think critically, write precisely, and realize how math applies to daily living, it is a good idea to begin to ask students to write their own story problems. A good homework assignment is to ask the children to "Write an addition and a subtraction problem using the numbers _____ and _____." This assignment can be given more than once by varying the numbers. Encourage the children to seek help from their parents.

Name _____

Directions: Read each problem. Then use the space by each
problem to draw a picture to show what the words
mean.

1. There are _____ rows.
   There are _____ desks
   in each row.
   How many desks
   in all? _____

2. You must read
   _____ pages.
   You have read
   _____ already.
   How many more
   must you read?

   _____

3. You have _____ eggs.
   You buy a dozen more.
   How many eggs do
   you have now?

   _____

© 1993 The Center for Applied Research in Education.

Name _____

Directions: Read each problem. Then use the space by each
problem to draw a picture to show what the words
mean.

1. _____ couples are
dancing.
How many people
are dancing?

_____

2. There are
_____ marbles.
Half are blue.
How many are
not blue?

_____

3. There are _____ stars.
There are _____ circles.
How many more
_____ than _____?

_____

Name _____

Directions: Read each problem. Then use the space by each
problem to draw a picture to show what the words
mean.

1. There are _____ teams.
   There are _____ children
   on each team.
   How many children
   are playing?

   _____

2. In a box, there
   are _____ candies.
   You ate _____.
   How many are left?

   _____

3. You collect _____.
   You have _____.
   For your birthday
   you got _____ more.
   Now you have

   _____ _____.

3–16 NUMBER PROBLEMS

Name _____

Directions: Read each problem. Then use the space by each
problem to draw a picture to show what the words
mean.

1. There are
   _____ children.
   There are
   _____ boys.
   How many are girls?

   _____

2. There are _____ boxes.
   There are _____ pens in
   each box.
   How many pens
   in all?

   _____

3. You have
   _____ dimes and
   _____ nickels.
   How much money
   do you have?

   _____

3–16 NUMBER PROBLEMS

Name _____

Directions: Read each problem. Then use the space by each
problem to draw a picture to show what the words
mean.

1. You have _____
   cookies to share with
   me. How many will
   each of us get?

   _____

2. There are _____ slices
   of bread. How many
   sandwiches can you
   make?

   _____

3. There are _____
   children and _____
   have to go home. How
   many are still playing?

   _____

© 1993 The Center for Applied Research in Education

Name _____

Directions: Read each problem. Then use the space by each problem to draw a picture to show what the words mean.

1. In a class there are _____ boys and _____ girls. How many students in all?

   _____

2. There are seven days in a week. There are _____ weeks until my birthday. That is _____ days.

3. On a plate, there are _____ apples, _____ oranges, and _____ plums. How many pieces of fruit are there?

   _____

Name _____

Directions: Read each problem. Then use the space by each
problem to draw a picture to show what the words
mean.

1. It is _____ o'clock
   now.
   What time will it be
   in _____ more hours?

   _____

2. In a box there
   are _____ candies.
   You decide to eat _____
   each day.
   How many days will
   the candy last?

   _____

3. Your brother is _____
   years old.
   You are _____ .
   How much older is he
   than you?

   _____

3–16 NUMBER PROBLEMS

© 1993 The Center for Applied Research in Education

Name _____

Directions: Read each problem. Then use the space by each
problem to draw a picture to show what the words
mean.

1. You have _____ pots.
   You want to
   plant _____ bulbs in
   each pot.
   How many bulbs will
   you need to buy?

   _____

2. You have _____
   quarters, _____
   dimes, _____
   nickels, and _____ pennies.
   How much money do
   you have in all?

   _____

3. You were born
   in _____. (list year)
   How old will you be
   in _____? (enter
   another year)
   I will be _____.

3–16 NUMBER PROBLEMS